CITIES OF THE DELTA, Part II

MENDES

AMERICAN RESEARCH CENTER IN EGYPT REPORTS

Preliminary and Final Reports
of Archaeological Excavations in Egypt
from Prehistoric to Medieval Times

Volume 5

Published under the auspices of
THE AMERICAN RESEARCH CENTER IN EGYPT, INC.

CITIES OF THE DELTA, Part II

MENDES

Preliminary Report on the 1979 and 1980 Seasons

by

Karen L. Wilson

Undena Publications
Malibu 1982

The seventh and eighth seasons of excavations at the site of ancient Mendes (modern Tell el-Rub'a) in the eastern central Delta took place during the summers of 1979 and 1980. The area chosen for excavation was a high ridge that lay outside and to the southeast of the Dynasty XXVI sanctuary enclosure and formed the south edge of what may have been a harbor of the ancient town. Excavation revealed that the ridge itself was probably built up by purposeful dumping of debris—of mixed Third Intermediate Period and Dynasty XXVI date—during the second half of the sixth century B.C. The building complex on the top of the ridge was preserved almost exclusively as foundations and included two structures containing domed cists that may have served as subterranean storage chambers. These complexes belong to a Late Period architectural type known from other Delta sites such as Memphis, Naukratis, Tell Defenneh, and Tell el-Maskhuta. The deep foundations of this complex had almost completely destroyed the remains of two earlier levels—one of which appeared to have been an industrial complex where faience objects were produced. To the north of these remains was a Late Hellenistic foundation system containing a series of rubble-filled chambers. The preliminary report of these excavations contains chapters on stratigraphy and architecture, pottery, Greek pottery, the various small finds, and a Third Intermediate Period relief fragment.

Library of Congress Card Number 81-52799

ISBN 0-89003-082-0 (paper)
0-89003-083-9 (cloth)

© 1982 by Undena Publications

All rights reserved. No part of this publication may be reproduced or transmitted in any form or by any means, electronic or mechanical, including photocopy, recording, or any information storage and retrieval system, without permission in writing from the author or the publisher.

Undena Publications, P. O. Box 97, Malibu, CA 90265, U.S.A.

CITIES OF THE DELTA

    With its close proximity to Palestine, Western Asia and the Mediterranean, the Nile Delta holds the keys to the solution of many fascinating problems in Egyptian history. Relatively little studied by the modern archaeologist, opportunities in this region have become easier to find and the amount of serious investigation has increased dramatically in recent years. The American Research Center in Egypt has sponsored three separate projects: Naukratis in the Western Delta, Mendes in the Eastern, Central Delta and Tell el-Maskhuta on the Ismailiya end of the Wadi Tumilat.

    Preliminary results of these three projects will hereafter appear under the common title: Cities of the Delta, although each separate report will contain the results of work at one site or one region only. In this effort to publish our findings in a timely fashion and in their support of the field projects themselves, we are grateful to the Smithsonian Institution which has been the financial backbone of so much of American archaeological work in Egypt. Other contributors and donors are credited in each of the individual reports.

Paul E. Walker
Executive Director
American Research Center
in Egypt

TABLE OF CONTENTS

LIST OF FIGURES viii

LIST OF ILLUSTRATIONS viii

1. INTRODUCTION – Karen L. Wilson 1

2. STRATIGRAPHY AND ARCHITECTURE – Karen L. Wilson 5
    Level I 5
    Level II 9
    Levels III, IV, V 11
    Squares X-XV 11

3. THE POTTERY – Susan J. Allen 13
    Method of Processing Pottery in the Field 13
    Fabric Typology 15
    Form Typology 17
    Late Hellenistic Pottery 18
    Late Period Pottery 19
    Third Intermediate Period Pottery 22
    Comparative Material 22

4. THE GREEK POTTERY – Marjorie Venit 27

5. VARIOUS FINDS – Karen L. Wilson 30
    Faience: amulets, figurines, and vessels 30
    Scarabs 33
    Terracotta amulet moulds 34
    Terracotta ram figurines 34
    "Tokens" 35
    Mitannian cylinder seal 35

6. A THIRD INTERMEDIATE PERIOD RELIEF FRAGMENT – Victoria L. Solia 37

7. CONCLUSIONS – Karen L. Wilson 39

LIST OF FIGURES

Figure

1. Key to balk drawings
2. Pottery type sheet
3. Pottery field recording sheet

LIST OF ILLUSTRATIONS

Plate	Illustration
I.	The Naos
II.	Master survey plan of Mendes
III.	Plan of Level I
IV.	Square IV, South balk
V.	Square II, Loci 3 and 2
VI.	Square I, East balk
VII.	Square II and northern portion of Square III, West balk
VIII.	1. Square III, Building D and Level IID wall
	2. Square IX, Building D
IX.	1. Square VII, Building D and Level IID wall
	2. Square VII, Building D, Locus 57
X.	Plan of Levels IIA and IIB
XI.	Plan of Levels IIC and IID
XII.	Squares X-XV, plan and East balk
XIII.	Late Hellenistic Pottery
XIV.	Bowls
XV.	Lamp, saucer, chalices, beakers, basins, and trays
XVI.	Elongated jars, globular jars, small jars, and Bes jar
XVII.	Holemouth jars and widemouth jars
XVIII.	Large jars and bottles
XIX.	Amphorae
XX.	Lids and burners
XXI.	Stands, miniatures, and theriomorphic vessel
XXII.	1. False spout of stirrup jar
	2. Shoulder fragment of "Rhodian" oinochoe
XXIII.	1. Shoulder and neck fragment of North Ionian vessel
	2. Shoulder fragment of "Rhodian" neck amphora
XXIV.	1-3. Three non-joining shoulder fragments of "Rhodian" neck amphora

List of Illustrations

Plate	Illustration	
XXV.	1, 2.	Mouth, neck and shoulder fragment of Clazomenian amphora
	3.	Body fragment of black figured vessel
XXVI.	1.	Body fragment of panel amphora
	2.	Bottom half of squat red figured lekythos
XXVII.	1.	Clazomenian amphora rim
	2.	Lekythos mouth and neck
	3.	Small olpe body
XXVIII.	1-13.	Faience *udjat*, Shu, Thoeris, hawk, ram and Thoth amulets
XXIX.	1-5.	Faience *uadj*, Pataikos, and Bes amulets
XXX.	1-3.	Faience vessels
XXXI.	1-3.	Scarabs
XXXII.	1-5.	Terracotta amulet moulds
XXXIII.	1-4.	Terracotta ram figurine fragments
XXXIV.	1.	"Tokens"
	2, 3.	Mitannian cylinder seal
XXXV.		Third Intermediate Period relief fragment

CHAPTER I

INTRODUCTION

Karen L. Wilson

The seventh and eighth seasons of excavations at the site of ancient Mendes (modern Tell el-Rub'a) in the eastern central Delta took place during the summers of 1979 and 1980. The seventh season was sponsored by the Institute of Fine Arts of New York University, the eighth season by the Smithsonian Institution, the Institute of Fine Arts, and the Seven-Up Bottling Company of Egypt. The excavations were conducted under the auspices of the American Research Center in Egypt.

The staff for the two seasons included: Bernard V. Bothmer and Donald P. Hansen, project directors; Karen L. Wilson, field director; Susan J. Allen, pottery specialist; James P. Allen, epigrapher; Lawrence Becker, conservator; Seitu Orondé, photographer; Victoria Landy Solia, registrar and archaeologist; Marjorie Venit, draftswoman and archaeologist; Laura Gadbery, Diana Hanson, Joan Huntoon, Sally Johnson, Joseph Josephson, Carolyn Kane, Alan Safani, and Helen Siegel, archaeologists. The representative of the Egyptian Antiquities Organization in 1979 was Ahmed el-Saroughi; in 1980, Ibrahim el-Sayyid.

In contrast to the narrow Nile Valley, the broad reaches of the Egyptian Delta contain numerous well preserved ancient town sites, and Mendes is one of the largest and best preserved of these mounds. It is the only site in the Delta currently being excavated that offers evidence of continuous occupation from the Archaic through the Ptolemaic Period. The history of the ancient town—a cult center and administrative capital—can be pieced together from written sources. Thus Mendes offers an unusual opportunity to study a major ancient Egyptian town both as it existed during specific periods and as it changed over the course of a long history. Excavation at Mendes also contributes to the increasing understanding of the Nile Delta, which was always of economic importance due to the fertility of its arable land, its extensive population, and its strategic geographic location, linking Northeast Africa with Western Asia and the Mediterranean world.

Throughout Egyptian history, Mendes occupied an important position as the capital of the Sixteenth Egyptian Nome and as the center of the cult of the local deity Banebdjed, the Ram.[1] Both inscriptional and archaeological evidence record a long and varied history for the site, dating back as far as the Archaic Period. The name Mendes itself is first mentioned in Fourth Dynasty texts. By Dynasty VI, probably as a result of the progressive

---

[1] A more detailed discussion of the history of ancient Mendes can be found in Herman DeMeulenaere and Pierre MacKay, *Mendes II* (Warminster: Aris and Phillips Ltd., 1976), pp. 172-181.

weakening of central power in Egypt, the town assumes historical importance. Middle Kingdom inscriptions have been found on the site, although occupation remains of this period have yet to be excavated. A foundation deposit found in secondary burial in the Saite temple provides evidence of Tuthmoside building on the mound, and Eighteenth Dynasty painted sherds—also excavated in secondary contexts—indicate that settlement of this period existed somewhere on the site. Fragments of inscriptions of Ramesses II and his successor, Merenptah, suggest that the kings of Dynasty XIX took an active interest in the city. Mendes is mentioned in several Third Intermediate Period inscriptions.[2] Around the year 804 B.C., the town became the seat of one of a number of local dynasties, the Chiefdoms of the Mă, whose rulers may have reigned until the first of the Twenty-sixth Dynasty pharaohs, Psamtik I. One of this king's successors, Amasis, constructed the great sanctuary with its massive red granite Naos, which still dominates the site (Pl. I). The Late Period city even became, albeit briefly, the capital of Egypt under the Twenty-ninth Dynasty. It continued as the capital of the Mendesian Nome throughout the Ptolemaic Period.

Six seasons of excavations at Mendes were funded by the Smithsonian Institution and conducted under the auspices of the American Research Center in Egypt during the summers of 1964, 1965, 1966, 1976, 1977, and 1978.[3]

A master survey plan of the site was completed during the first season (Pl. II). The preserved portion of the mound covers an area of just over ninety hectares and rises to a maximum height of about thirteen meters above the surrounding fields, or 17.68 m. above sea level. As the map shows, the tell is divided into two major parts, which contain archaeological remains of two different types. The temple precinct, on the northwest, is bounded by massive mud brick enclosure walls slightly less than two kilometers in perimeter. Within the temple enclosure stands the red granite Naos of Amasis (Pl. I, II:A)—almost all that remains of the great Twenty-sixth Dynasty sanctuary. Numerous fragments of ram sarcophagi are scattered throughout the area, having been exposed and dislodged by the diggings of the local *sebbakhin*. North of the Naos are the exposed remains of limestone tombs of the Sixth Dynasty (Pl. II:B), and the entire enclosure is dotted with the disintegrating rubble of stone buildings of undetermined date. Southeast of the Naos are private houses and traces of numerous ovens that may mark the site of the temple bakeries (Pl. II:D).

In contrast, the whole vast southern portion of the mound is densely covered with mud brick architecture, often extensively exposed by the *sebbakhin*. This appears to have been the main residential and industrial quarter of the Late Period town. Along the western and southern fringes of the kom, as defined by the modern cultivation, are the kiln areas of the settlement.

---

[2] K.A. Kitchen, *The Third Intermediate Period in Egypt (1100-650 B.C.)* (Warminster: Aris and Phillips Ltd., 1973), pp. 345, 366, 392-393, 402.

[3] For reports of the work of these seasons see: Donald P. Hansen, "Mendes, 1964," *JARCE* 4 (1965), pp. 31-37, and "Excavations at Mendes, 1965-1966," *JARCE* 6 (1967), pp. 5-16; Christine L. Soghor, "Inscriptions from Tell el-Rub'a," *JARCE* 6 (1967), pp. 16-32; Edward L. Ochsenschlager, "Excavations at Thmuis," *JARCE* 6 (1967), pp. 32-52; Karen L. Wilson, "Excavations at Mendes in the Nile Delta, 1976-1979," forthcoming in *Actes du IIème Congrès International des Égyptologues*; "Tell el-Robaa (Mendès)," *Orientalia* 48 (n.s.) (1979), pp. 346-347.

1. Introduction

From 1964 to 1978, work concentrated primarily on the Saite sanctuary precinct, which was expected to be the oldest and most continuously occupied portion of the mound. Excavation in the immediate vicinity of the Naos revealed an elaborate foundation system, designed to support the weight of a total of four monolithic red granite naoi. The foundations of the Amasis temple had cut down some eleven meters into a First Intermediate Period cemetery, which lay just above a series of Old Kingdom mastabas (Pl. II:C). Below the forepart of the Saite temple were a number of Sixth Dynasty tombs of a different type, consisting of a long shaft descending to an elaborately painted limestone burial chamber (Pl. II:B). Apparently as the result of extensive erosion, these tombs—which were originally underground—now stand exposed on the present surface of the mound.

Although inscriptional material found within the precinct attested to continuous settlement at Mendes during the Middle and New Kingdoms, occupation levels of these periods were not preserved in the areas excavated. Therefore, almost nothing could be learned of the nature or extent of settlement at the site during almost a millennium and a half of a history in which the eastern Delta often played a critical role.

This significant gap could be filled in only by excavating a series of occupation levels that spanned these intervening periods. Thus the primary goal of the seventh season of excavations at Mendes was to locate an area of the mound that could be expected to yield the desired chronological range of materials. If a settlement sequence extending from the Archaic through the Late Period could be completed, it would provide a picture of the total history of Mendes and a series of dating criteria for less securely stratified remains from heavily *sebbakh*ed portions of the kom. Such material would also prove useful to excavators working in the Delta on sites where a similarly long sequence of occupation does not exist or has not yet come to light.

A second goal of the season was to investigate an area that lay outside the great enclosure walls of the sacred precinct. If excavation in such a place yielded remains of a non-sacred, non-funerary nature, it would provide material evidence of a type not obtained previously for Mendes.

At the beginning of the 1979 season, several high rises on the southern portion of the mound were sherded with a view toward locating an area that seemed likely to yield a long series of occupation strata extending back in time from the Twenty-sixth Dynasty. The ridge chosen for excavation, situated roughly at S100-170, E200-320 (Pl. II:H), appeared to have terminal occupation of the late sixth century B.C. and included the highest preserved point on the mound (S150.05, E296.69), which stood 17.68 m. above sea level. Therefore, the area seemed likely to yield the desired sequence above either the present sub-surface water table (at approximately 2.50 m. above sea level) or virgin soil. Of added interest was the fact that this high rise extends along the south edge of a large depression that one geological study has indicated was a harbor of the ancient town (Pl. II:I).[4] There was, therefore, good reason to expect that settlement in the area had been of a commercial or industrial nature.

---

[4] M.A. el-Sharkawi, *The Geology of Tell el-Rub'a; Results of the 1978 Summer Investigations* (unpublished manuscript, Institute of Fine Arts, New York University, 1979).

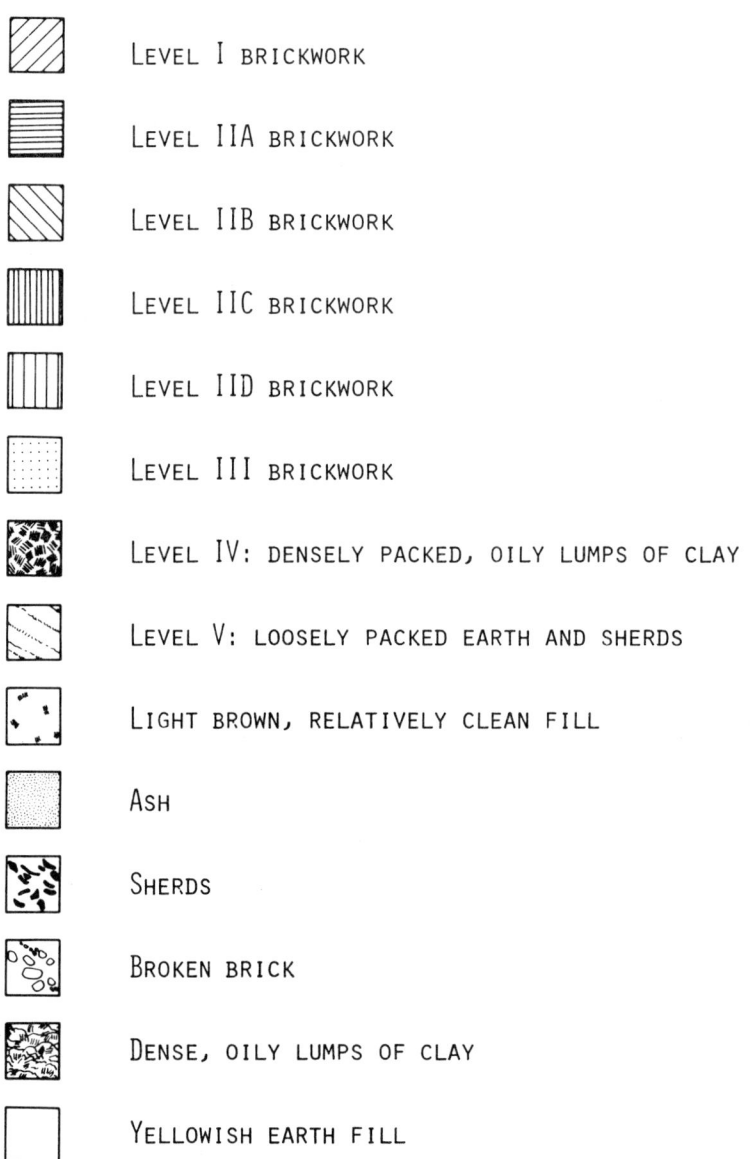

Figure 1. Key to balk drawings.

CHAPTER 2

STRATIGRAPHY AND ARCHITECTURE

Karen L. Wilson

Level I:

Although most of the southern portion of the mound of Mendes has been robbed extensively by the local *sebbakhin*, the area chosen for excavation had remained virtually untouched. It soon became clear that this unusual state of preservation resulted from the density of the mud brick structures preserved just below the surface (Pl. III).[1]

Remains of three closely contemporary buildings constituted the first level. These consisted primarily of a series of deep foundations, including a number of domed cists that may have served as subterranean storage chambers. In most cases, only the foundations were preserved and the exterior floor levels of the structures had weathered away along with the surface of the mound. Thus, few stratigraphic links could be established among the buildings. All the evidence recovered indicates, however, that the various structures of Level I must have been built within a relatively brief span of time and were all in simultaneous use for at least part of their history.

The northern complex consisted of a row of square chambers (Building A) flanked on the east and west by nearly solid mud brick platforms (Buildings B and C, respectively). Buildings A and B were set in a single foundation trench, which cut the foundation trench of the slightly earlier Building C (Pl. IV). The later foundation trench was sunk deeper below the walls than it was within the doorless chambers and in the corridor between the two structures, creating internal floor levels at the height of the fifth course of brickwork. No exterior floors were preserved. The bricks used in Buildings A and B were light in color and sandy in consistency, and measured 34-41 x 18-22 x 9-13 cm.

---

[1] It should be noted that true north is 22° counter-clockwise from the north-south grid lines shown on all the plans. The reason for this discrepancy is as follows: All the survey points established during the making of the master survey plan of the site (Pl. II) have disappeared within the past sixteen years with the exception of two British survey markers: B_1 (N196.98, E7.26, within the precinct enclosure) and A_4 (N507.28, E68.87, next to the modern road north of the precinct enclosure). The coordinates of these points could not be carried over the high enclosure wall to the area of the 1979-1980 excavations prior to the onset of work, so a grid was laid out in the area with a simple compass orientation to north, and excavation preceded within that grid. Squares were numbered with Roman numerals in the order in which they were opened (the square number is shown in the lower left hand corner of each square). When the coordinates were later carried over to the excavated area, the new grid was found to deviate 22° toward the east from true north. The true grid will be superimposed on the new one during the coming year and all field records will be adjusted accordingly.

The highest preserved portion of the mound above these buildings was over the west half of Loci 2 and 3. There the lower portions of part of the domed roofs of these two chambers were preserved (Pl. V). The domes were constructed in a simple manner by stepping in successive courses of brickwork—first over the corners of the rooms to form pendentives, then in the superimposed circular courses of the dome itself. The rooms to the north were probably similarly roofed, but the mound sloped down sharply at that point to a level well below what would have been the springing of the domes. One chamber (Locus 48) retained traces of a mud plaster coating on the walls.

The fill of these chambers provided no firm evidence as to their original function—whether they were designed for storage or a structural purpose.[2] The contents varied from chamber to chamber and consisted of debris dumped in as a purposeful fill either at the time of construction or after the cists had passed out of use.

The walls of Building A were poorly constructed, with little mortar in the vertical joints, and would seem to have been structurally incapable of serving as a support for an overlying building. The more solid mud brick platforms to the west and east, however, could have provided a foundation for some type of superstructure. The excavated portion of Building B was solid mud brick except for one open chamber (Locus 34), which contained a dense sherdy fill.

Building C lay parallel to Building A and the north edges of both structures were on the same line. However, as stated above, the foundation trench of A and B cut that of C, indicating two different phases of construction.

The bricks of Building C consisted of a dark brownish-gray clay with almost no straw or other tempering material. While damp they formed a cohesive structure, but after exposure to air and sun, they crumbled and broke apart. The bricks were laid with a layer of hard, light mortar, varying from 3 to 7 cm. in thickness, between each course. Often a layer of reeds had been laid either below or above the mortar (a practice also in evidence in Building B). There was no mortar in the vertical joints. Brick sizes varied, but fell within two main groups: 41-42 x 20-25 x 10-13 cm. and 35-38 x 11-23 x 7-13 cm.

Building C was constructed as follows (Pl. VI-VII). The bottom of the foundation trench was first filled with 20 to 60 cm. of pure, yellowish earth. Above this fill, the lowest courses of brick were laid. Seven courses formed the south and east edges of the structure, then an eighth, levelling course was added where necessary to create a perfectly horizontal surface. The space between the brickwork and the edge of the foundation trench was then filled with earth and capped by a stepping out of the overlying courses of brickwork.

The portion of Building C excavated in the west half of Square I rested directly on an earlier structure of nearly solid mud brick (Pl. X). During the digging of the foundation trench for the west portion of C, the east edge of the earlier structure was cleared down to its base. The lowest eight courses of the Level I brick stopped in a vertical face 98 to 38 cm. east of this edge. The intervening space (Locus 36) was filled with loose rubble and capped by the upper courses of the terrace, which continued over the whole Level IIB structure.

---

[2] Because the 1980 season ended after the beginning of the Moslem fasting month of Ramadan, it was not possible to arrange for an immediate division of the scientific samples which are to be brought back to New York for analysis—and which should shed some light on the function of these chambers. An application has been submitted to the Department of Antiquities for such a division.

Within the fabric of the lower courses of Building C were several chambers (Loci 17, 23, 37, 38). The sides of these chambers varied in height from two to six courses, they were filled with the same pure, yellowish fill as the bottom of the foundation trench and were capped by the upper courses of the building. Locus 38, which lay within the balk between Squares I and II, had a brick bottom on the west side (Pl. VI) and a layer of reeds laid about half way up on the east side (Pl. VII).

Adjacent to and within the balk between Squares I and II there was a chamber of a different type (Locus 24), which extended up to the preserved top of the brickwork. The bottom of this chamber consisted of one to two courses of brick, with reed matting and a few pottery vessels above. At the preserved top of the chamber in Square I was a globular vessel covered by a second layer of reeds.[3] Two similar chambers to the north (Loci 50 and 39) contained fairly clean debris.

Due to the denudation of the upper portions of Buildings B and C, it is not possible to determine the purpose of these chambers. They may have corresponded to the placement of overlying rooms or may have had a structural function.

To the south of this complex was a fourth building (D), which was similar in many respects to those to the north but was more carefully and solidly constructed. Building D was a nearly perfect square, measuring approximately 11.00 m. on a side. It was constructed of bricks of the same sizes as those used in the other buildings, laid in alternate header-stretcher courses in a very hard, sandy mortar. Light colored, sandy and dark, clayey bricks—apparently made of materials coming from two different sources—were mixed in the fabric of the structure.[4]

The exterior walls of the building were carefully constructed to direct the thrusts of the weight of the mud brick toward the center of the massive structure (Pl. VIII-IX:1). Each wall had a pronounced inward batter from bottom to top, and the courses of each side of the building were laid with a pronounced downward slope toward the center. The brickwork was reinforced by the insertion of hardwood beams,[5] averaging 12 cm. in diameter, in horizontal rows perpendicular to the facade and diagonally into the corners.

Most of what survived of Building D was subterranean; but exterior, living floors (Loci 18, 51, and 67) and roughly ten courses of the superstructure were preserved on all four sides. A narrow wall ran parallel to the north and east edges of the building. This wall was set within the foundation trench itself and was preserved eight to ten courses in height. A series of untamped earth floors had accumulated in the narrow corridor between this wall and Building D. The west and south ends of this wall were cut by later brickwork, and there was no evidence of similar walls to the west or south of the building.

The south facade of Building D was preserved to a maximum height of ten courses and had a 5 cm. thick coating of mud plaster (Pl. VIII:2). The plaster extended down over a tamped earth floor, which sloped down slightly to the south across the area excavated.

---

[3] These vessels were one of type 7MP188 (Pl. XV:2), one of type 7MP367, and 7MP17 (Pl. XVI:4).

[4] The mixing of these two different types of bricks in the same structure is also seen in the sanctuary enclosure wall and in many of the large buildings exposed by the *sebbakhin* on the southern portion of the mound and may eventually prove to be a valid means by which to date these structures.

[5] The analysis of the wood samples was conducted by the Center for Wood Anatomy Research, U.S. Forest Products Laboratory, Madison, Wisconsin.

Lying on this floor were a number of whole vessels and two deposits of pot sherds re-worked into disc shaped "tokens" or counters.[6]

Three irregularly shaped buttresses had been erected against the southern half of the west facade of the building after the accumulation of about 20 cm. of earth floors. One of these earlier floors yielded a worn clay document seal[7] and several whole vessels of the same type as those found to the south of the building.

The foundations of Building D were approximately 2.50 m. deep. The foundation narrowed toward the bottom (Pl. VIII:2 and IX:1) so that it was exactly the size of the building at its lowest course.

Building D contained nine subterranean chambers irregularly arranged in three parallel rows of three. Complete domes, with an 80 cm. circular opening in the center, were preserved in four chambers (Loci 22, 21, 57, 72) (Pl. IX:2). There was evidence of collapsed domes in four other chambers (Loci 68, 71, 69, 47). Only Loci 21 and 47 were cleared completely. There was no evidence of a doorway or doorways in either chamber. The bricks were laid in alternating header-stretcher courses. Ten to twelve courses from the bottom (at a height of just under 1.50 m.), the springing of the dome began, constructed in the same fashion as those in Loci 2 and 3. Each dome was six courses high. The top of the dome (which was on approximately the same level as the lowest external floor of the building) was covered with mud plaster that extended down over the edges of the central opening. Above the domes, the walls continued up in line with the walls of the chamber below and were preserved to a maximum height of twelve courses. Irregularly spaced in these upper walls were what appeared to be holes for reinforcing beams smaller than those visible on the outer walls of the building, but no traces of wood were found in any of these holes.

The fill of these chambers was, once again, apparently not indicative of their original function—unless they were designed simply as rubble-filled foundation chambers for a more elaborate superstructure, a function seemingly belied by the careful plastering of the domes. The fill consisted of clean earth (and, in Locus 47, collapsed mud brick from the dome) plus a number of large worked limestone slabs and basin fragments, broken faience vessels and amulets, and considerable quantities of pottery. The fill below and above the domes was the same, suggesting a purposeful filling of the entire structure to its preserved height. There was no evidence of floors of any kind above the domes.

During a slightly later phase of Level I, a room (Locus 5) containing three large clay ovens (Loci 6, 9, 7) and a pottery vat in the northeast corner was built up against the north "enclosure" wall of Building D. The ovens were used repeatedly, and a large deposit of ash accumulated around them and within the room above the original tamped earth floor. The ash, in alternating layers of red and black, contained slag, sherds, and carbonized organic material.

The three ovens were roughly ovoid in plan, tapered slightly toward the top, and were preserved to finished edges between 45 and 60 cm. in height. Each oven stood over a pit

---

[6] The pottery consisted of carinated bowls (cf. Pl. XIV:6, 7, 10), a high necked jar (cf. Pl. XVI:3), and a number of examples of type 7MP117 (Pl. XVII:6). For a discussion of "tokens" see p. 35.

[7] 8M86. The impression is badly worn and has not yet been read completely.

approximately 25 cm. deep which had the sides, but not the bottom, fired like the oven itself. There was no evidence of stoke holes in any of these pits, which suggests that they may have served only for the original baking of the clay ovens, which were later fired through the opening at the top.

Level II:

Beneath and badly cut by the Level I structures were four strata comprising disconnected architectural remains and an apparent industrial layer of large vats, worked limestone fragments, and pits filled with ash and slag. Because of the homogeneous character of these remains and associated artifacts, and because the levels were badly cut so that no single stratum yielded a coherent plan within the excavated area, all were designated Level II and that level was subdivided into four main stratigraphic phases.

Level IIA (Pl. X) was a stratum at least partly formed during the course of industrial activity centered on the manufacture of faience objects. A dozen terracotta amulet moulds and numerous faience objects—amulets (including types that match the moulds), beads, vessel fragments, and scarabs—came from this level along with a profusion of such artifacts as conical limestone objects, limestone basins, fragmentary metal implements, and pot sherds re-worked into disc-shaped "tokens."[8] The excavated portion of this stratum contained almost no architecture but had been an outdoor area. Its remains consisted primarily of a series of large pottery vats, burning pits, and extensive deposits of ash and slag cut down into Level IIB.

In the southeast portion of Square II and the north half of Square III, Level IIA comprised a series of large pottery vats and smaller pottery vessels surrounded by deposits of densely packed clay and sherds. A dozen complete or nearly complete vessels—some standing upright and others apparently inverted—were found stacked one above the other in Square II, Locus 4.[9] (The positions of vessels in the uppermost layers are marked A-G on Pl. X). One of these vessels—the lower half of an ovoid jar with a rounded base—contained three small juglets, fifty-nine pottery "tokens," two white stone "tokens," an egg-shaped quartzite grinder, and two conical pieces of limestone.[10] The surrounding debris consisted primarily of crude splintered potsherds, which may indicate that one of the activities in this area was the reworking of pot sherds into tokens. A brick platform, only one course high, projected from the east balk of the square just north of these vessels. To the south (Locus 26) were the lower portions of several large vats surrounded by fragments of worked limestone and baked brick. The bases of these vats were sunk into the Level IIB walls and surrounded by dense clay that enabled them to stand upright.

The west portion of Square III (Locus 44) and the east half of Square V (Locus 40) appear to have been the oven area of this industrial quarter. The debris here consisted

---

[8] See pp. 30-35 for a discussion of some of these objects.

[9] These vessels included one of type 7MP563 (Pl. XVIII:2) and two pots of similar form, one of which had three handles; two examples of type 7MP457 (Pl. XVIII:3), and type 7MP564 (Pl. XVI:1).

[10] See Pl. XXXIV:1.

primarily of repeated lenses of dark ash, often mixed with pockets of slag. Two large circular ovens (Loci 10 and 11) were so poorly preserved that little can be said about their construction or method of use. In addition to these two ovens, all of Loci 40 and 44 was pockmarked with small burning pits, without preserved superstructures, which had been sunk into the debris at various levels during the course of its accumulation. Several large pottery jars and vats (A-D), sunk into the Level IIB walls and into a deep deposit of dense clay that covered the northwest corner of Square V (Locus 15), were similar to those from Squares II and III. Similar vessels in Squares IV and IX probably belong to the same level.

Level IIB consisted of architectural remains and associated occupation strata unevenly preserved within the excavated area. Cuts from above Level I, the excavations for the foundations of the Level I structures, and Level IIA had destroyed most of the plan of IIB and the majority of the stratigraphic links between the different portions of this level.

A massive wall, badly cut by Level IIA and later pits, lay within and to either side of the balk between Squares I-II and V-III. The wall was constructed of sandy yellow bricks with fine straw temper, averaging 36 x 11 x 9 cm. in size, laid in a thick, hard mortar nearly identical in composition to the bricks.

Alternating layers of clean fill and deposits of whole and fragmentary vessels lay against the north face of this wall in Locus 1. The vessels were mixed with ash, bone, slag, pottery "tokens," and occasional faience amulets and shells, and the entire deposit had the character of a gradual accumulation of dumped debris, rather than a purposeful fill.

The east end of this wall abutted on, but was not bonded to, a wider wall or building founded on exactly the same level and constructed of the same type of bricks. The plan of this structure had been almost completely destroyed by Level IIA.

In the southwest portion of Square V were remains of narrow walls enclosing three rooms (Loci 12, 13, 14), which originally must have been part of a building that extended toward the southwest. The east edge of this structure had been completely cut away by the burning pits of IIA.

To the northwest of Locus 1 was a nearly solid mud brick platform that extended outside the excavated area to the north and west. This structure was built of typical Level IIB sandy, yellow, straw tempered bricks, measuring 36 x 17 x 10 and 35 x 11 x 7 cm., laid in alternating header-stretcher courses with an extremely hard, cream-colored mortar.

The excavated portion of this platform had one rectangular chamber near the center (Locus 8) filled with an ashy red fill and fragments of baked brick. This debris probably reflects a secondary use of the structure or chamber, as a large cut (Locus 8W) in the western portion of the brickwork contained a similar ashy fill. Within the fabric of the structure itself were a plastered buttress east of Locus 8 and a long, narrow chamber (Locus 8E) filled with clean earth fill.

Levels IIC and D appear to be the uppermost layers of a series of fills that may largely, if not wholly, constitute the high rise under investigation during 1979 and 1980. The architectural remains associated with these various strata are enigmatic not only because the Level I foundations destroyed much of their plan, but also because they are not associated with any preserved occupation remains.

Level IIC was sealed by a layer of densely packed sherds, which lay under the massive Level IIB wall and the structure abutting it on the east. This sherd layer is visible on the sections (Pl. VI-VII) just under, and cut into by, that wall.

2. Stratigraphy and Architecture

A scrap of east-west wall only four courses high in Squares I and II, a piece of north-south wall in the southwest quarter of Square I, and the northern half of a circular oven in Square II (Pl. XI) comprise the Level IIC architectural remains. Associated with these fragments of brickwork is a layer of dense, oily lumps of clay containing some sherds, which slopes down sharply to the south (Pl. VI and VII). This stratum lenses out within a layer of light orangish fill that lies up against and extends under two Level IID structures in squares V, III, and VII.

The Level IID structures were badly cut by later levels, so that little evidence of their original function was preserved. As excavated, they appear to have been constructed simply to contain a purposeful stratum of fill.

The building in Square V was preserved to a maximum height of ten courses and its east end was completely cut away by the Level IIA burning pits. The structure consisted of a square chamber on the west (Locus 33) separated by an unbonded cross wall from what may have been a similar chamber (Locus 35) to the east.

The second structure, which had a slightly different orientation, was almost completely destroyed by the foundations of the Level I Building D (Pl. IX:1). The north facade had a pronounced inward batter from bottom to top and, on the east half, the lowest eight courses of brickwork projected slightly beyond those above (Pl. VII and VIII:1). Little else can be said about this structure except that the interior may have been subdivided into rooms or chambers by unbonded cross-walls in a manner similar to the building to the west.

Levels III, IV, V:

The lowest three levels reached in the course of the excavation were all purposeful fills without associated architectural remains (Pl. VI). The lowest stratum (Level V), probed only in a small sounding in the northeast corner of Square I and exposed over a very limited area, consisted of loosely packed earth and sherds deposited at almost a 45° downward slope from north to south. Above this was a layer roughly one meter thick of dense, oily lumps of clay, which followed the same slope. The top surface of this layer had been smoothed carefully before the overlying Level III was deposited. This stratum consisted primarily of a strikingly homogeneous loose, pink-gray fill, apparently with a high ash and pulverized slag content. Interspersed within this primary fill type were small lenses of broken mud brick. Each lense seemed to represent a single unit of deposition (perhaps a basket, on analogy with modern Egyptian practices). The bottom of Level III sloped at a sharp angle, following the upper surface of Level IV; near the top, the tip lines were somewhat less steep.

Squares X-XV:

When the sounding in Square I reached a total depth of 7.00 m., it became too dangerous to continue excavating due to fall from the tops of the north and east balks, which had weathered badly during the previous winter. As the size of the labor force and the amount of time remaining in the 1980 season would not permit widening the upper edges of the sounding for safety, the decision was made to try to reach and understand the underlying strata by a different means.

The north edge of the ridge directly north of Square IV was cut by a wadi which ran down toward the north into the "harbor" depression. The excavation area was extended to the north by opening a line of two 10.00 x 10.00 m. squares and four 5.00 x 10.00 m. squares within the wadi to take advantage of the cutting already accomplished by extensive erosion (Pl. XII). It seemed likely that work in these new squares would consist of tracing the opposite slope of the fill layers (running this time down from south to north) and might reach the thinner outer edges of these fills, beneath which earlier strata might be accessible.

However, the six new squares incorporated, almost exactly, the north-south extent of a Hellenistic foundation system built of mud brick and cut down into the Level III debris. Unfortunately, the excavated portions of these foundations yielded almost no information concerning the type of structure to which they had belonged.

The foundations measured approximately 45.00 m. from north to south and contained seven irregularly placed rectangular chambers filled with loose earth, ash, sherds, and fragments of terracotta figurines. Two larger chambers, containing similar fill, were visible in the east section of the wadi. The two "walls" which defined the south chamber were each only one brick wide.

The south edge of the structure was traced to a depth of 6.00 m. below the surface but neither its bottom nor the bottom of the Level III debris was reached. The base of the north edge of the foundations, at an absolute level of 4.60 m. above sea level, rested on Level I-II type deposition, which extended down for a meter and a half and disappeared under the present sub-surface water table.

CHAPTER 3

THE POTTERY

Susan J. Allen

The diversity of pottery found during the seventh and eighth seasons was remarkable. The area excavated—just over 1200 square meters—yielded approximately 1150 identifiable pottery types. These types divide into four chronological groups: Ptolemaic, Late Period (Dynasties 26-30), Third Intermediate Period (Dynasties 22-25), and New Kingdom (Dynasties 18-21).

Method of Processing Pottery in the Field

All ceramic material collected on the excavation was transported daily to the excavation house, where it was washed and analyzed. The system of recording used had been developed over the course of the previous six seasons.[1]

Rather than immediately try to correlate the forms found this season with those from previous seasons' work elsewhere on the site, it seemed preferable to formulate a new corpus of types and to use this to record the new material while in the field.[2] First, a working typology of the different fabrics was made. Each fabric type was further subdivided by surface treatment (none, wet smoothed, slipped, burnished, or painted). Nondiagnostic body sherds were counted and recorded according to this fabric typology.

Diagnostic sherds (profiles, rims, bases, handles, spouts) and decorated body sherds were recorded as types defined on the basis of both morphological attributes and fabric.

---

[1] This system was developed by Edward Ochsenschlager (Brooklyn College) and Donald P. Hansen (Institute of Fine Arts, New York University) during the course of excavations at Mendes (1964-66, 1976-78) and at al-Hiba, Iraq (1967-1974). The goal of the system is complete recording of all available ceramic data in an internally consistent form geared to formal, statistical, and technical analyses subsequent to the field season (see Edward L. Ochsenschlager, "The Mendes al-Hiba System of Pottery Classification," *Studien zur ägyptischen Keramik*, Deutsches Archaeologisches Institut, forthcoming).

[2] Most of the Late Period pottery from Mendes was excavated during the first three seasons, and the type sherds deteriorated badly during the ten year hiatus in the excavations following the 1967 war. Because the recording procedure depends on comparison of newly excavated sherds with already existing type sherds, as will be described below, the condition of the old type series posed a serious problem. Although drawings of the sherds did exist, the use of them for typing purposes proved to be too cumbersome. It was therefore decided to formulate a new type series which could be correlated with the older one after the end of the season.

3. The Pottery

MENDES EXPEDITION

Pot Type _____   Pottery Number _____   Catalogue Number _____

Date of Finding	Period	Locus	Neg. No.	☐ Whole
Area		Coordinates	Drawn	☐ Fragment
		Level	Disposition	☐ Reconstructed

Height
Diameters:
.... Rim
.... Body
.... Base
Normal Thickness:
Special measurements:

Form
Rim
Handle
Base

☐ Hand made
☐ Wheel made
☐ Mold made
☐ Heavily fired
☐ Moderately fired
☐ Lightly fired
☐ Warped

☐ Poorly made
☐ Fairly well made
☐ Well made
☐ Very well made

Paste
Color range

☐ Grit temper
☐ Plant temper

Density
☐ Sparse
☐ Medium
☐ Heavy
Color of inclusions

Inclusions
☐ Fine _____
☐ Medium _____
☐ Coarse _____
☐ Very coarse _____

☐ Granular
☐ Laminated
☐ Dense
☐ Friable

Surface
Color range
Luster range

☐ Smooth
☐ Rough
☐ Granular

Treatment
☐ None
☐ Wet-smoothed
☐ Self-slip
☐ True-slip
☐ Wash
☐ Glaze
☐ Burnish

Condition
☐ Even
☐ Uneven
☐ Abrasing
☐ Peeling
☐ Crazing
☐ Scaling

Decoration

Findspot & Associations

Remarks & Bibliography

Figure 2. Pottery type sheet.

3. The Pottery

The new corpus of types was built up by comparing the diagnostic sherds to one another; each new and definable form was assigned a type number.[3] The same form occurring in two different fabrics was assigned two separate type numbers (this was rare). Variations in surface treatment or decoration did not affect the type designation.

As new types were defined, the representative sherds were laid out on large tables and grouped by shape—bowls, wide mouthed jars, amphora bases, etc.—so that new material could be compared easily with them. If a better preserved or more complete example of a type was found, it was substituted for the "type sherd" on the table. Each type was recorded on a special form (Fig. 2), fully described, and drawn. Selected pieces were photographed.

A basket or baskets of sherds from a particular day and locus were handled as follows. The sherds were washed and sorted into diagnostic and nondiagnostic groups. Nondiagnostic sherds were divided by fabric and then by surface treatment, counted, and recorded on a specially printed form according to the portion of the vessel from which they came (neck, shoulder, belly, or other) (Fig. 3). Diagnostic sherds were compared to the type corpus. If a sherd matched an already existing type, it was recorded on the printed form by type number, along with measurements of preserved height and diameter and description of fabric and surface treatment. If a sherd could not be matched with any of the types on the tables, it became a new type and was assigned a type number, noted on the recording sheet, and placed in the type corpus. All decorated sherds, both diagnostic and nondiagnostic, were noted on the sheets and set aside for subsequent stylistic examination. Sherds coming from the same locus, but on different days, were recorded as separate groups.

Greek pottery was recorded separately.[4] Every fragment was assigned a number, all diagnostic sherds were drawn, and all decorated material was drawn and photographed.

It should be emphasized here that this process created a working typology, subject to constant modification. Types were dropped if they turned out to be aberrations or nonsignificant variants from the norm of an already well defined type. If two type features—a rim and a base, for example—were found to belong to a single vessel shape, they were reclassified under a single type.

Fabric Typology

The fabric types identified divide into two basic groups: those made from alluvial clays and those made from marl clays. Alluvial clay fabrics fall into two major and two minor groups. The first major type is a reddish brown, basically organic tempered fabric, which also contains a small proportion of finely crushed limestone (?) and is usually low to moderately fired. The second is a hard, fine textured, well fired fabric containing a

---

[3] Each pottery type number is composed of four elements: 1) the number of the season during which the type was defined, 2) a capital M for Mendes, 3) a capital P for pottery, 4) the type number. Thus the first type defined in 1979 was 7MP1, the second type was 7MP2, and so on. A separate type series was established for the Greek pottery and the types were designated 7MPX1, 7MPX2, and so on.

[4] See pp. 27-29 for a discussion of this material.

MENDES EXPEDITION

No. of Pages	Date	Area	Coordinates	Locus	Level
Page No.	Feature and Location			Fieldbook page	

	Profiles	Rims	Necks	Shlders	Bellies	Bases	Handles	Spouts	Indist.	Fab.	Treatment		
1. Statistics											Int.	Ext.	Dec.
2. Profiles	Type	Diam.	Pres. Ht.	Recognizable Form									
3. Bases													
4. Rims													
5. Handles, Spouts													
6. Striking Variants, New Types													

Characterization of Assemblage

Comments

Initials

Figure 3. Pottery field recording sheet.

mixture of finely divided organic material (such as dung) and grit—which might be fine sand, grog (ground sherds), or crushed limestone (?). The two minor types are a very fine textured, hard, grit tempered, well fired red fabric and a black fabric with a black burnished slip. Both are confined to the Ptolemaic Period types.

The marl clay fabrics divide into those that fire pinkish and those that have a greenish tinge. Both types are grit tempered, sometimes with grog made from red alluvial clay fabrics. Although the basic clay material of both types is fine textured, the density of the pastes varies according to the grade and type of temper material. Some of the pinkish fabrics are very gritty (tempered with coarse sand or crushed limestone), while the greenish fabric is often spongy and probably had an organic temper. In general, however, the fineness of both the clay and temper creates a hard, compact fabric with a relatively smooth surface.

Simple visual analysis in the field was undoubtedly insufficient for the identification of all imported marl clay fabrics or of those fabrics composed of a mixture of marl and alluvial clays. Such information should be revealed by technical analyses, to be conducted during the coming year.

A ware classification combining fabric and surface treatment with shape will be established during the coming seasons. Surface treatments of alluvial fabrics include wet smoothing, slips (red and white), a thin white wash, and a combination of slipping and burnishing, usually with streaky or circular strokes. The marl clays may be washed or slipped or burnished, but normally the surface of the fabric is so smooth that it requires little additional treatment, except occasional wet smoothing. The pinkish marl clays, especially, develop a whitish film on their surfaces during firing, which gives them a slipped appearance.

Few of the sherds are decorated. The most common type of decoration is plastic: applied bands of clay which are notched or pinched to give a scalloped effect; applied knobs and ribs; and incised, applied, and pinched faces on Bes jars (Pl. XVI:10). The most elaborate examples of painted decoration seem to be imported from elsewhere in the Mediterranean.[5]

Form Typology

A systematic typology based on the morphology of the forms will be made after a larger pottery corpus is compiled. At present, the types have been divided provisionally into several basic groups, a summary of which is presented here. The plates illustrate a representative sample of some of the most common and best preserved types. The Key to the Plates gives the provenience and a description of basic vessel shape, fabric, surface treatment, and decoration, plus the dating of the type. The terminology used is based primarily on that of Shepard, Nordstrom and Holthoer.[6] The color designations are those of the Munsell Soil Color charts.[7]

[5] *Ibid.*

[6] Anna O. Shepard, *Ceramics for the Archaeologist* (Washington, D.C.: Carnegie Institution of Washington, Publication 609, 1954), pp. 95-305; Hans-Ake Nordstrom, *Neolithic and A-Group Sites* (The Scandinavian Joint Expedition to Sudanese Nubia, Vol. 3) (Stockholm: Scandinavian University Books, 1972); Rotislav Holthoer, *New Kingdom Pharaonic Sites: The Pottery* (The Scandinavian Joint Expedition to Sudanese Nubia, Vol. 5, Part 1) (Stockholm: Scandinavian University Books, 1977).

[7] Munsell Soil Color Charts. 1973 edition. Macbeth Division, Kollmorgen Corp., Baltimore, Md.

The provisional type groups are:

I. Open Forms (Unrestricted)
    A. Bowls
        1. Straight or slightly concave profiles, usually with a flat base
        2. Carinated profiles with flat or round bases
        3. Straight, concave, or carinated profiles with pointed bases
    B. Lamps and saucers
    C. Chalices and beakers (a category which also includes some closed forms)
    D. Basins
    E. Trays

II. Closed Forms (Restricted)
    A. Jars
        1. Elongated
        2. Globular
        3. Small
        4. Bes
        5. Holemouth
        6. Widemouth
        7. Large
    B. Bottles
    C. Amphorae

III. Other Forms
    A. Lids
    B. Burners/Braziers
    C. Stands
    D. Miniatures
    E. Theriomorphic vessels

All together, eighty types are illustrated on the plates. Of these, twenty-seven are open forms, thirty-eight are closed, and fifteen fall into the category of other forms. Most of the types are made from alluvial clay fabrics and are wheelmade.

Late Hellenistic Pottery (Pl. XIII)

The pottery corpus from the Hellenistic foundations in Squares X-XV is characterized by ring base bowls with incurving rims (Pl. XIII:1, 3); ring base jugs (Pl. XIII:5); a variety of amphora base types (e.g. Pl. XIII:8-9); and wide mouthed cooking pots with sharp, angular profiles, horizontal loop handles, and an interior rim ledge to hold a lid (Pl. XIII:4). Black burnished and hard, fine grained red wares are common.

3. The Pottery 19

The material compares well with that excavated during the fifth season at Kom el-'Izam, which lies directly across the flat depression to the north of the current excavation (Pl. II:G,[8] and with the corpus of Late Hellenistic pottery from ancient Thmuis (modern Tell Timai).[9]

Late Period Pottery (Pl. XIV:1, 5-11; XV:1-9; XVI; XVII:1-7, 9-10; XVIII:2-7; XIX-XXI)

The greatest proportion of types in the corpus come from Levels I-II and are datable to the Late Period. The open forms display a preference for flat, string cut bases or slightly rounded, scraped bases; while the closed forms usually have rounded bases, often with a small nipple in the center.

Carinated bowls (Pl. XIV:6-11) are one of the commonly found forms diagnostic of this period. The majority of these bowls are shallow with flat or slightly rounded bases, although a few deeper types also occur. Carinated bowls show two basic vessel profiles: one with a sinuous contour in which the carination occurs above the midpoint (Pl. XIV:6-8) and another in which the carination occurs below the midpoint and forms a sharp corner from which the vessel wall continues upward in a straight line (Pl. XIV:9-11).

Deep bowls with a flat base, straight divergent sides—usually ribbed at wide intervals—and a folded over or thickened rim are one of the most common bowl types made of marl clay (Pl. XIV:1). The fabric varies from coarse and spongy to reasonably dense. This type of bowl, and that illustrated in Pl. XIV:5, may have been used as lids.[10]

Small hemispherical bowls with a thick red burnished slip (Pl. XV:1) constitute a frequent and standardized form. The rims of these bowls are usually blackened with soot, indicating that they were used as lamps. The interiors are often incised after firing (right through the slip and into the fabric itself) with a design or owner's mark, some of which are repeated on a number of lamps.

Chalices or footed goblets with disk or spool bases and convex or straight divergent profiles (Pl. XV:3-4) are also diagnostic of these levels. Beakers such as the one shown on Pl. XV:5 (which is actually a closed form) are common while a finer type (Pl. XV:6) with a thick, lustrous red slip occurs less frequently.

A large number of vats or basins and large heavy trays are included among the open forms. Pl. XV:7 shows the most common basin form; often the rim of this type is decorated with a broad band of clay which is notched or scalloped. A class of trays represented here by one example (Pl. XV:9) have broad ledge rims and sometimes have a heavy ring base or three large feet, rather than the flat base reconstructed here.

Jars characteristic of the Late Period corpus include long, sausage shaped jars, most of which narrow towards the midpoint and have nippled bases and short, nearly vertical necks (Pl. XVI:2). The type illustrated in Pl. XVI:3 is found with both a plain and ribbed

---

[8] Personal communication from Edward Ochsenschlager.

[9] Edward L. Ochsenschlager, "Excavations at Thmuis," *JARCE* 6 (1967), pp. 34-51.

[10] Personal communication from Helen Jacquet-Gordon. However, if the bowl type shown in Pl. XIV:1 were used as a lid, it would be rather difficult to grasp.

(Pl. XVI:5) neck. Globular jars (Pl. XVI:4, 6) have a variety of rim and neck forms and are usually red slipped and burnished. Pl. XVI:7-9 shows three small jars of types that often survived intact. Two discovered inside the remains of a large ovoid jar may have been dipper juglets.

Pl. XVI:10 shows one of three nearly complete Bes jars excavated during the two seasons. The others were large storage jars similar in form to the vessel illustrated on Pl. XVIII:4. Bes jar fragments were fairly common and exhibited a wide range of pinched, modelled, applied and incised faces, and varied greatly in size.

Wide mouthed forms were a common and diverse group. The type shown in Pl. XVII:6 was probably the most common form found in the Late Period levels. A variant form survived into the Ptolemaic Period (Pl. XIII:7). Two vessel types (Pl. XVII:4-5) are similar in shape to the later Hellenistic cooking pots (Pl. XIII:4), but are less angular and have only simple rims. They are normally red slipped, only moderately fired, and show no signs of blackening. Pl. XVII:7 shows a diagnostic Late Period type which was also found at Mit Rahineh.[11]

Large "storage" jars (Pl. XVIII:3-4) were usually found in fragmentary condition. The type illustrated on Pl. XVIII:4 was the most common. Those examples discovered *in situ* were held upright by a dense packing of clay or mud brick around the base.

Bottle types varied greatly from one to the other and tended to occur as unique examples. One interesting type, which was common and easily identifiable from even small fragments, is shown in Pl. XVIII:7. This pilgrim bottle was made of a hard pinkish fabric and seems to have been formed in two halves over a cloth covered mold. The interiors of body sherds from this type preserve distinct impressions of the weave of the cloth and even of seams showing the pattern of the sewing thread. The neck and rim were made separately and the three pieces were joined together; the longitudinal joint was concealed with a strip of clay that was brought up to form two tiny loop handles. In shape and construction, these pilgrim bottles are strikingly similar to the faience New Year's bottles also found in these levels, although the pottery examples are not inscribed or decorated with floral designs.[12]

Amphorae constitute the bulk of the pottery types that were made of marl clay fabric. It is often difficult, on the basis of visual analysis alone, to determine which of these types were made locally and which were imported. The most frequent forms are neckless amphorae with a short, nearly horizontal shoulder, two small opposed twisted handles, and a long body ending in a pointed base (Pl. XIX:1-2). Though well thrown and fairly uniform in size, they are carelessly finished, and many show marks of wear on the interior of the rim: grooves or scored areas that appear to have been created by cords rubbing against or over them. Similar vessels are commonly found in Iron II levels in Palestine,[13] as well as elsewhere in Egypt.

---

[11] See the list of comparative material, p. 25.

[12] See p. 33 and Pl. XXX:3.

[13] Ruth Amiran, *Ancient Pottery of the Holy Land* (New Brunswick, N.J.: Rutgers University Press, 1970), pl. 79:2; Photo 246; pl. 81:4-7; pl. 82:6. The Mendes examples are made of a fabric visually similar to that of the Palestinian ones, which is described by Amiran (p. 241) as "well levigated and well-baked to give off a metallic sound, and is yellowish-pink in color."

3. The Pottery

The painted amphorae (Pl. XIX:3-4) are a type which Petrie called "Chiote" in his publication of the material from Tell Defenneh and Naukratis.[14] The cream colored slip of the Mendes examples is slightly chalky, in contrast to the usual thick, hard slips of Chiote wares; the decoration is a free form, loop design in thin red paint.

A common type of large, heavy and coarse lid is illustrated on Pl. XX:7. These lids are usually recovered in fragments, separated from their handles, which are a pinched strap rather than a true loop handle. The underside of this example is rough, cracked, and pitted, indicating that it probably was formed directly on the ground or some other uneven surface. It has been suggested that this type of lid was used to cover bread ovens similar in form to those found in Locus 5.[15]

Other lids (Pl. XX:1-6) are similar in form to bowls and saucers, but sometimes have a slight groove or projection on the rim to hold them in place and are blackened on the interior edges, presumably because they were used to cover cooking pots on the fire. The diameters of small cup lids (Pl. XX:1-4) indicate that they could have been used to cover narrow necked jars similar to those illustrated on Pl. XVI:1-3, 5.

The two illustrated examples of "burners" (Pl. XX:8-9) may have been used for incense. Both show traces of burning only on the interior of the rim. The type shown in Pl. XX:9 has an exact parallel at Mit Rahineh.[16]

A large variety of stand fragments—usually bases—were found during the two seasons. The type shown on Pl. XXI:3 was ubiquitous in the Late Period levels. The illustrated example was the most common variant, but there were also two decorated types with incised and applied decoration, as well as small models of these types. Other excavators have published these stands with the legs pointing downward,[17] but examination of hundreds of examples from Mendes has shown this to be untenable. The "legs" curve inward so that the vessel is unstable when resting on them, and the inner edges of the tips of these "legs" are bevelled inward. The flat surface is extremely rough, still bears the impression of the surface it rested on while being made or while drying, and is usually concave. Most examples are provided with two ledge handles angled so as to be functional only if the vessel were lifted with the "legs" pointing upward. All these features make the type well suited for use as a stand, perhaps to catch drips from a vessel (like a modern *zir*) resting on it. The fact that none of the numerous pieces found showed any traces of burning indicates that they were not braziers or stoves.

Small ring stands of the type shown on Pl. XXI:1 were also common. The larger example with a bowl (Pl. XXI:2) was relatively rare.

A limited number of theriomorphic and miniature vessel types were defined. Nearly all of them appeared only once. Theriomorphic vessels included several types of birds (e.g. Pl. XXI:6) and a bottle in the form of a human figure wearing a wide knee length

---

[14] See the list of comparative material, p. 25.

[15] Personal communication from Helen Jacquet-Gordon. Henry Fischer, "Pottery," in Rudolf Anthes, et al., *Mit Rahineh 1955* (Museum Monographs) (Philadelphia: The University Museum, 1959), pp. 30-31.

[16] See the list of comparative material, p. 26.

[17] e.g. Rudolf Anthes, et al, *Mit Rahineh 1956* (Museum Monographs) (Philadelphia: The University Museum, 1965) pl. 66 no. 614. However, Fischer notes in the text (p. 157) that the drawing is probably inverted and that vessels of this type may have been used as stoves.

cape. The miniature forms—a group defined by size rather than morphology—comprised bowls (Pl. XXI:4), bottles (Pl. XXI:5), amphorae, and stands. None of these types was functional and they varied from very rough, schematic pieces to carefully executed examples.

Third Intermediate Period Pottery (Pl. XIV:2-3, 12-13; XV:10; XVII:8, 11; XVIII:1)

The bulk of the Level III-V pottery is datable to the Third Intermediate Period but may include some Late Ramesside material. The predominant ware is a hard, dense, well fired, grit tempered alluvial clay fabric, which is more finely levigated and better fired than most of the Late Period wares. The Third Intermediate Period pottery is characterized by the continuation of shapes which began in the New Kingdom and were originally produced in a much softer fabric.

The assemblage of forms is much less diverse than that of the Late Period. Bowl and cup types (Pl. XIV:2-3, 12-13) tend to be deep with pointed or rounded bases. They are usually carefully smoothed but unslipped. Coarse, hand made types, which occur in a variety of forms during the Late Period, are rare in these levels. Small, shallow trays (Pl. XV:10) occur fairly commonly, with minor variations in profile. They resemble modern Egyptian plates (called *dokkas*) on which the dough for making sun-raised bread is placed.[18] Wide mouthed jars with folded over or thickened rims (Pl. XVII:8, 11; XVIII:1) and high vertical necked jars with marked ribbing on the interior characterize these levels. These types are covered with a matte slip, or a thick lustrous cream slip, or a thin smeary white wash applied in a visually pleasing, streaky pattern.

A few examples were found of types which are common at Upper Egyptian sites in pre-Twenty-sixth-Dynasty contexts. Almost all were made of marl clay fabric. These types include sinuous-sided carinated bowls, ovoid jars with ribbed bodies and maximum diameters below the mid-point, and short cut and modelled jar rims. The fact that so few examples of these types were found, and that marl clay wares formed a proportionally small part of the Mendes ceramic corpus, may indicate that this group were imports from Upper Egypt.

Comparative Material

Parallels for thirty-seven of the seventy-one Third Intermediate and Late Period types illustrated are given in the list of Comparative Material. These parallels are drawn primarily on the basis of shape, as most older publications have inadequate descriptions of ware or fabric, if any at all. The parallels listed tend to be for the most distinctive types. The more complex forms—such as incense burners and stands—are more often published and provide more secure comparative data than, for example, simple bowls, the fabric of which tends to vary over time whereas the forms have a chronologically longer range.

---

[18] Personal communication from Helen Jacquet-Gordon.

3. The Pottery

The comparative material ranges in date from Dynasty XVIII to Ptolemaic times. Most of the parallels falls into the period from the Twenty-second to Thirtieth Dynasty.

The comparisons indicate that the rather extensive corpus of Mendesian Third Intermediate and Late Period pottery seems to belong to a Lower Egyptian tradition that probably did not extend much farther south than Memphis. This tradition is related to Upper Egyptian material in the general lines of its development, the perpetuation of older forms in the Third Intermediate Period, and the wholesale introduction of new forms at the time of the Twenty-sixth Dynasty. However, individual forms and the frequency of their appearance are different in the two parts of Egypt.

24   *3. The Pottery*

COMPARATIVE MATERIAL

PLATE XIV

1. 7MP418   Petrie, W.M. Flinders, et al. *Naukratis. Part I. 1884-5.* (Third Memoir of the Egypt Exploration Fund) (London: Trübner and Co., 1886), pl. 4:2, ca. 650 B.C.
    Petrie, W.M. Flinders. *Hyksos and Israelite Cities* (British School of Archaeology in Egypt, and Egyptian Research Account, 12th year, 1906) (London: British School of Archaeology in Egypt, 1906), pl. 39F:134, Dynasties 26-30.
    Petrie, W.M. Flinders, and Mackay, Ernest. *Heliopolis, Kafr Ammar and Shurafa* (British School of Archaeology in Egypt, and Egyptian Research Account, 18th year, 1912) (London: British School of Archaeology in Egypt, 1915), pl. 10:2.

4. 7MP581   Petrie, *Hyksos Cities*, pl. 21A:10, Ptolemaic and Roman.

7. 7MP596   Jacquet-Gordon, Karnak Nord Type 596 (unpublished), Ptolemaic-Roman.

11. 7MP316 Petrie, *Hyksos Cities*, pl. 20A (no number), Dynasty 26.
    Petrie, W.M. Flinders. *Qurneh* (British School of Archaeology in Egypt, and Egyptian Research Account, 15th year, 1909) (London: British School of Archaeology in Egypt, 1909), pl. 54:815, Dynasties 23-26.
    Petrie, *Heliopolis*, pl. 33:11, Dynasties 23-25.
    Petrie, W.M. Flinders, et al. *Tanis. Part II. Nebesheh (Am) and Defenneh (Tahpanhes)* (Fourth Memoir of the Egypt Exploration Fund) (London: Trübner and Co., 1888), pl. 35:79, 600-550 B.C.

12. 7MP388 Petrie, *Tanis II*, pl. 3:29, Dynasties 25-27; pl. 19.
    Petrie, *Hyksos Cities*, pl. 36B:9.
    Petrie, W.M. Flinders, et al. *Lahun II* (British School of Archaeology in Egypt, and Egyptian Research Account, 26th year, 1920) (London: British School of Archaeology in Egypt, 1923), pl. 59:6M, Dynasties 22-24.
    Anthes, Rudolf, et al. *Mit Rahineh 1956* (Museum Monographs) (Philadelphia: The University Museum, University of Pennsylvania, 1965), pl. 62:549, Dynasty 22.
    Brunton, Guy. *Matmar* (British Museum Expedition to Middle Egypt, 1929-1931) (London: Bernard Quaritch, 1948), pl. 57:6E, Dynasties 22-25.

13. 7MP510 Anthes, Rudolf, et al. *Mit Rahineh 1955* (Museum Monographs) (Philadelphia: The University Museum, University of Pennsylvania, 1959), fig. 7:71.
    Anthes, *Mit Rahineh 1956*, pl. 62:506, Dynasty 22.
    Petrie, *Hyksos Cities*, pl. 36B:10, 13, 15, 16.

PLATE XV

3. 7MP102   Petrie, *Lahun II*, pl. 59:13J, K, Dynasties 22-24.
    Petrie, *Heliopolis*, pl. 33:26, 28, Dynasties 23-25.
    Petrie, *Tanis II*, pl. 35:40.

6. 7MP103   Petrie, *Tanis II*, pl. 35:78, Dynasty 26.
    Petrie, *Qurneh*, pl. 54:816, Dynasties 23-26.

8. 7MP508   Jacquet-Gordon, Karnak Nord Type 584 (unpublished), Dynasty 25?

10. 7MP149 Ibid., Type 65, Dynasties 21-Ptolemaic?
    Brunton, *Matmar*, pl. 57:1D, H, Dynasties 22-25.

PLATE XVI

1. 7MP564   Petrie, *Hyksos Cities*, pl. 39F:156, Dynasties 26-30.
    Petrie, *Lahun II*, pl. 59:45G, Dynasties 22-24.

Plate XVI (cont.)

2.	7MP61	Petrie, *Qurneh*, pl. 51:811, Dynasty 22.
3.	7MP94	Petrie, *Hyksos Cities*, pl. 39F:159, Dynasties 26-30. Petrie, *Tanis II*, pl. 5:29, Dynasty 26, Amasis II. Anthes, *Mit Rahineh 1955*, fig. 3:32.
5.	7MP81	Petrie, *Hyksos Cities*, pl. 20A:410, Dynasty 26. Petrie, *Heliopolis*, pl. 34:56-57, Dynasty 23 or later.
6.	7MP585	Petrie, *Heliopolis*, pl. 11:38, Dynasties 19-26.
7.	7MP48	Petrie, *Hyksos Cities*, pl. 36B:29. Petrie, *Tanis II*, pl. 35:74, end of the 6th century B.C.
9.	7MP434	Petrie, *Qurneh*, pl. 54:840, Dynasties 23-26. Brunton, *Matmar*, pl. 57:82Q, Dynasties 23-25.
10.	7MP186	Petrie, *Heliopolis*, pl. 11:48, Dynasties 19-26.

PLATE XVII

5.	7MP16	Petrie, *Hyksos Cities*, pl. 21A:13, Ptolemaic. Petrie, *Qurneh*, pl. 54:819, Dynasties 23-26. Petrie, *Heliopolis*, pl. 33:15, Dynasties 23-25.
6.	7MP117	Petrie, *Hyksos Cities*, pl. 21A:11, Ptolemaic; 36A:2-3, probably Dynasty 26; pl. 39H: 251, 263, Ptolemaic. Petrie, *Heliopolis*, pl. 33:32, Dynasties 23-25.
7.	7MP233	Anthes, *Mit Rahineh 1955*, fig. 4:34, Graeco-Roman? Anthes, *Mit Rahineh 1956*, pl. 57:402, 403; Graeco-Roman.
8.	7MP657	Jacquet-Gordon, Karnak Nord Type 585 (unpublished), Dynasties 18-20.
9.	7MP88	Anthes, *Mit Rahineh 1956*, pl. 59:405, Late.
11.	7MP624	Jacquet-Gordon, Karnak Nord Type 716 (unpublished), Dynasties 26-Ptolemaic.

PLATE XVIII

2.	7MP563	Anthes, *Mit Rahineh 1955*, fig. 2:18.
7.	7MP6	Petrie, *Tanis II*, pl. 35:67. Anthes, *Mit Rahineh 1956*, pl. 61:458, Late.

PLATE XIX

1.	7MP39	Petrie, *Qurneh*, pl. 51:798. Petrie, *Heliopolis*, pl. 11:34, probably Dynasty 22.
2.	7MP72	Petrie, *Hyksos Cities*, pl. 36A:7, probably Dynasty 22. Petrie, *Tanis II*, pl. 33:4, ca. 650 B.C.
3.	7MP459	Petrie, *Tanis II*, pl. 36:5, Dynasty 26, Amasis II. Petrie, *Naukratis I*, pl. 16:4, Dynasty 26.

PLATE XX

2.	7MP707	Petrie, *Heliopolis*, pl. 33:22, Dynasties 23-25.
3.	7MP758	Anthes, *Mit Rahineh 1955*, fig. 10:84.
4.	7MP765	Jacquet-Gordon, Karnak Nord Type 727 (unpublished), Dynasties 26-Ptolemaic.
7.	7MP38	Anthes, *Mit Rahineh 1956*, pl. 66:612.

3. The Pottery

Plate XX (cont.)

9. 7MP18   Petrie, *Tanis II*, pl. 35:77.
   Petrie, *Heliopolis*, pl. 11:51, Dynasties 19-26.
   Anthes, *Mit Rahineh 1955*, fig. 11:85.
   Anthes, *Mit Rahineh 1956*, pl. 67:609-610, Dynasty 22.

PLATE XXI

1. 7MP104   Petrie, *Tanis II*, pl. 34:33.

3. 7MP11   Petrie, *Tanis II*, pl. 33:9, ca. 650 B.C.
   Petrie, *Heliopolis*, pl. 11:53, Dynasties 19-26.
   Anthes, *Mit Rahineh 1956*, pl. 66:614.

4. 7MP60   Anthes, *Mit Rahineh 1956*, pl. 64:605, Late.

CHAPTER 4

THE GREEK POTTERY

Marjorie Venit

The imported pottery excavated at Mendes during the seventh and eighth seasons includes a number of fragments of Mycenaean ware and over one hundred pieces of Greek pottery from the archaic and classical periods. Unfortunately, none of this pottery was found in a primary context. The Mycenaean sherds all came from Level III. With few exceptions, the seventh and sixth century Greek pottery came from the sherd layer of Level IIC, while the later Greek fragments were found on or near the surface, in areas disturbed in antiquity.

A body sherd with spiral decoration, the foot and lower body of a globular vessel, and the false spout of a stirrup jar (Pl. XXII:1) constitute the Mycenaean finds.

The Greek pottery ranges in date from the seventh through the mid-fourth century B.C. The earlier pottery was imported almost exclusively from the East Greek cities on the west coast of Anatolia and the nearby islands. Later finds, the earliest of which date to the first quarter of the sixth century, are consistently Attic.

The earliest piece of Greek pottery—a fragment from the shoulder of a "Rhodian" vessel, probably an oinochoe[1]—preserves part of a file of water birds (Pl. XXII:2). The remains of three birds are visible: at the right of the fragment is the wing of the leading bird, at the left of the fragment, the beak of the third. This fragment belongs to the Middle Wild Goat II style and should date to the last quarter of the seventh century B.C.[2]

A fragment from the shoulder of a neck amphora (Pl. XXIII:2) is also "Rhodian." It comes from a late type of vessel whose decoration is limited to a single goat, his head turned back, on either shoulder.[3] A companion vessel is represented by three non-joining fragments which also preserve gamboling goats (Pl. XXIV:1-3). On the largest fragment (Pl. XXIV:1), the turn of the goat's head is indicated by the tip of his beard, which is preserved above his back. These three fragments are slightly different from the first in thickness, profile, and color, yet the similar scheme of decoration connects the two vessels closely. The two Mendes amphorae are paralleled among vases excavated at Tocra, in

---

[1] Compare, for example, Rhodes 12219, *Corpus vasorum antiquorum*, Italy 9, II Dh 4:1.

[2] For a discussion of Middle Wild Goat II and its dates see R.M. Cook's review of Chrysoulas Kardara, *Rhodiaki Angeiographia* (Bibliotheke Archaiologike Hetaireia 49) (Athens, 1963) in *Gnomon* 37 (1969), pp. 502-507, especially p. 506. Cook's suggested dates are used here.

[3] Kardara, *Rhodiaki Angeiographia*, pp. 209-210, fig. 180.

modern Libya.⁴ The similarity in the form of the vessels, the style of the animals, and the sparse filling ornament suggest that these vases may all proceed from the same workshop. Like the Tocra vases, the Mendes amphorae should be dated 580-560 B.C.

Contemporary with the last two vessels from Mendes is a fragment of a ware quite commonly exported to Egypt in antiquity (Pl. XXIII;1).⁵ The homeland of this ware, which was once considered to be of Rhodian origin, is now sought farther north and, although a specific city-state is still unidentified, the fabric is now generally referred to as North Ionian.⁶ This ware is characterized by a thick, soapy slip, paint firing to red, heavy filling ornament, much added red, and incision which does not stop at merely clarifying inner details but often reiterates the contour of the painted decoration. On the Mendes piece, this latter characteristic may be seen in the incision of the central palmette. The shapes most frequently encountered in this fabric are kraters with ring handles and bowls. The Mendes fragment is unusual, although not unique,⁷ not only because it probably represents a neck amphora, but also because it carries a figurative frieze on the neck, as well as on the shoulder.

Clazomenian ware, which also found a ready market in Egypt,⁸ is represented at Mendes by two fragments from a large neck amphora (Pl. XXV:1 and XXVII:1; Pl. XXV:2). The large size of the Mendes rim fragment, the profile of its lip, the checkers on its edge, the sphinxes or sirens on its neck, and its plastic fillet closely connect this piece with a nearly complete amphora—once in Berlin, but lost in the second world war—which was purchased at Benha, a town about forty kilometers southwest of Mendes.⁹ The second fragment from the Mendes vessel reiterates the relationship with the Benha amphora, for it repeats in all details the cocks seen on the shoulder of the more complete vase. The only difference is the disposition of the added color on the tongues above. There can be no question that the two vases are by the same hand, and one might propose that they were painted within a short span of time and even brought to Egypt aboard the same ship. The correct interpretation of the proximity of their findspots should help shed light on the pottery trade between Greece and Egypt in the sixth century B.C. The fragments by the Painter of the Benha amphora may be dated 550-540 B.C. and are the latest East Greek fragments found at Mendes.

⁴ John Boardman and John Hayes, *Excavations at Tocra 1963-1965: The Archaic Deposits I* (The British School of Archaeology at Athens, Supplementary Volume No. 4) (Oxford: Thames and Hudson, 1966), pl. 28, no. 580, 581 and p. 4, n. 7. The first vase is cited by Elena Walter-Karydi, *Samische Gefässe des 6. Jahrhunderts v. Chr.* (Deutsches Archäologisches Institut, Samos Band VI¹) (Bonn: Rudolf Habelt, 1973), p. 144, no. 929 as North Ionian, but this is unlikely.

⁵ Much has been found at Naukratis, e.g. Cairo 26.139, CC. Edgar, *Catalogue général des antiquités égyptiennes du Musée du Caire: Greek Vases* (Cairo: L'Institut Francais d'Archéologie Orientale, 1911), pl. 2; Cairo 26.160, Cairo 26.161.

⁶ See Boardman, *Tocra I*, p. 64; Walter-Karydi, *Samos VI¹*, pp. 77-80 for the probable homeland of this ware.

⁷ Compare Syracuse 33847, *Samos VI¹*, pl. 109, no. 907.

⁸ See list of proveniences in R.M. Cook, "A List of Clazomenian Pottery," *The Annual of the British School at Athens* 47 (1952), pp. 148-149 and "Bedeutung der bemalten Keramik für den griechischen Handel," *Jahrbuch des Deutschen Archäologischen Instituts* 74 (1959), p. 117.

⁹ Berlin 4530. Walter-Karydi, *Samos VI¹*, pl. 127, no. 919. Unfortunately, the vessel was lost during World War II (personal correspondence from Dr. Elisabeth Rohde, Director, Staatliche Museen zu Berlin).

4. The Greek Pottery

The earliest Attic ware found at Mendes dates ca. 580-570 B.C. and, like the contemporary East Greek fragments, comes from an animal style vase (Pl. XXV:3). On the upper frieze, a feline strides to the right; only his legs and underbelly are preserved. In the lower frieze, an animal—probably a deer or a goat—grazes to the left; only his shoulder is preserved. Since Attic vases were exported to Egypt as early as ca. 600 B.C.,[10] this Mendes fragment represents the second generation of Attic potters whose work is found in Egypt. The second fragment of Attic black-figure pottery (Pl. XXVI:1) is from a panel amphora and preserves only two feet, moving to the right, with a bit of drapery between them. This fragment may just post-date the Persian conquest of Egypt in 525 B.C. and, if so, would be one of the few pieces of Attic pottery from this period found in Egypt.[11]

Much of the fifth century Attic pottery is represented solely by tiny fragments, which offer little criteria for close dating. The earliest clearly datable piece—a body fragment from a cylindrical pattern lekythos with ivy and korymboi—should be placed in the second or third quarter of the century.[12] The most common import into Egypt in the late fifth and early fourth century, however, was the squat lekythos. At Mendes more than a dozen fragments of this shape, both decorated and black glazed, have been identified with certainty. The most complete example (Pl. XXVI:2) preserves a crouching sphinx, her paw raised.

Most of the fifth and fourth century Attic fragments come from small shapes. Besides lekythoi (Pl. XXVII:2), cups and an olpe (Pl. XXVII:3) may be identified.

Among published sites, Mendes is fourth behind Naukratis, Defenneh, and Memphis in the number of fragments of Greek pottery excavated, yet at Mendes there is no independent evidence, whether archaeological, epigraphical, or textual, for Greek habitation. Since the corpus of this pottery from Mendes is relatively small and comes only from secondary context, it would be premature at this point to draw conclusions concerning the reasons for its presence at the site.

---

[10] The earliest Attic vases found in Egypt are from the time of the Gorgon Painter.

[11] I welcome the opportunity to thank Mary B. Moore for looking at the Attic fragments with me.

[12] 8MPX51. For this dating see Donna C. Kurtz, *Athenian White Lekythoi: Patterns and Painters* (Oxford: Clarendon Press, 1975) caption for pl. 70, 6 (second through third quarter of the fifth century) or, alternately, second half of the fifth century (p. 154).

CHAPTER 5

VARIOUS FINDS

Karen L. Wilson

Plates XXVIII-XXXIV illustrate representative examples of the most common types or classes of objects and a few unusual pieces found during the 1979 and 1980 seasons. All these finds are small in size and very few of them are inscribed. The bulk of the material consists of what are generally broadly referred to as "Late Period" types and are not more specifically datable within that time span on the basis of parallels with other excavated or unexcavated objects.

Faience: amulets, figurines, and vessels (Pl. XXVIII-XXX)

Faience objects constituted the largest single category of finds. Most of the pieces were small amulets and vessel fragments; larger figurines and complete or reconstructable vessels were rare. The glaze, when preserved, varied in color from deep to pale blue and green, with occasional details picked out in dark or yellowish brown.

Thoeris amulets were the most frequently found type. They varied from small, schematic representations (Pl. XXVIII:10)—the most common form—to carefully modelled figurines seven or eight centimeters tall. The thirty examples excavated were fairly evenly distributed among Levels I-III; none occurred in Levels IV-V or in the Late Hellenistic foundations.

Pl. XXVIII:9   7M136. Square I, Locus 43, Level IIC. Thoeris amulet: blue glazed faience; suspension loop at top of back pillar. H=3.80 cm.

Pl. XXVIII:10 7M26. Square I, Locus 1, Level IIB. Thoeris amulet: blue glazed faience; pierced behind head for suspension. H=3.10 cm.

The second most common amulets were *udjat* eyes. Pl. XXVIII:1-2 illustrate the standard type, which may be either one or two sided, with plain or hatched brow, a raised pupil (often covered with a dark brown glaze), and incised eyelids and falcon markings. Most are pierced lengthwise for suspension; rare examples have a cylindrical suspension loop at the top. Twenty-two amulets of this type came from Levels I-II; none occurred in either the Hellenistic foundations or Levels III-V.

5. Various Finds

Multiple *udjat* amulets with a central eye (Pl. XXVIII:6) were one of the types manufactured in Level IIA. Two identical examples and the mould in which they were made (Pl. XXXII:1) were found in Square V, Locus 15; a third amulet came from Square III, Locus 44.

Pl. XXVIII:1   7M7. Square III, surface. *Udjat* amulet: pale blue glazed faience; pierced lengthwise for suspension; features incised; raised pupil with dark glaze. L=2.10 cm.

Pl. XXVIII:2   7M34. Square V, Locus 12, Level IIB. *Udjat* amulet: blue glazed faience; pierced lengthwise for suspension; features incised; raised pupil with green glaze. L=1.60 cm.

Pl. XXVIII:3   7M89. Square V, Locus 14, Level IIB. *Udjat* amulet: blue glazed faience; pierced lengthwise for suspension; features on obverse raised and marked with brownish-yellow glaze; features on reverse incised. L=1.50 cm.

Pl. XXVIII:4   7M153. Square VI, in bricks of Building B, Level I. *Udjat* amulet: faience, no traces of glaze; pierced lengthwise for suspension; schematic features incised on obverse and reverse. L=1.55 cm.

Pl. XXVIII:5   7M139. Square I, Level III. *Udjat* amulet: pale green glazed faience; pierced lengthwise for suspension; cornea in openwork. L=1.70 cm.

Pl. XXVIII:6   7M130. Square V, Locus 15, Level IIA. Multiple *udjat* amulet: pale blue glazed faience; pierced lengthwise for suspension; central eye motif and two *udjat*s above and below. H=1.80 cm.

Shu amulets were the third most common type found in Levels I-II; none occurred in either Levels III-V or the Late Hellenistic foundations. Twelve examples of carefully modelled amulets (Pl. XXVIII:7), ranging in height from 1 to 4 cm., came from Levels I-II. Fifteen "hieroglyphic" Shu amulets, in which the representation was reduced to a single plane and executed with incised details (Pl. XXVIII:8), were limited to Level II.

Pl. XXVIII:7   7M132. Square II, Locus 2, Level I. Shu amulet: light blue glazed faience; back pillar pierced for suspension. H=3.25 cm.

Pl. XXVIII:8   7M41. Square II, Locus 4, Level IIA. Shu amulet: pale blue glazed faience; back pillar pierced for suspension. H=2.30 cm.

Uadj amulets in blue and green glazed faience were another common type. Eight examples with carefully executed papyriform capital and striated suspension loop (Pl. XXIX:2) occurred in Levels I-IIB. Twelve amulets of a more schematic and less graceful type (Pl. XXIX:1) were found in Levels I-IIC.

5. Various Finds

Pl. XXIX:1   7M116. Square V, Locus 43, Level IIC. *Uadj* amulet: pale blue glazed faience; suspension loop at top. H=3.80 cm.

Pl. XXIX:2   7M36. Square I, Locus 1, Level IIB. *Uadj* amulet: blue glazed faience; striated suspension loop at top. H=3.80 cm.

Pataikos amulets (Pl. XXIX:3) occurred in all levels. They ranged from extremely small, schematic pieces to well executed examples. Bes amulets (Pl. XXIX:5) were less common; most were smaller and coarser than the one illustrated here. Pataikos amulets stood on a rectangular base and had a suspension loop at the back of the neck; Bes amulets had a back pillar pierced for suspension and no base. Three superbly modelled, headless figurines of bandy-legged dwarfs standing on rectangular bases were identified tentatively as representing Pataikos (e.g. Pl. XXIX:4).

Pl. XXIX:3   7M40. Square II, Locus 4, Level IIA. Pataikos amulet: blue glazed faience, suspension loop at back of neck. H=3.20 cm.

Pl. XXIX:4   7M74. Square III, Locus 19, Level I. Headless figurine of bandy-legged dwarf (Pataikos ?): light blue glazed faience. H=4.70 cm.

Pl. XXIX:5   7M138. Square VI, Locus 42, Level IIA. Bes amulet; faience, no traces of glaze; back pillar pierced for suspension. H=2.80 cm.

Other amulet types, all of which occurred only in Levels I and II, include the gods Thoth (Pl. XXVIII:13) and Anubis; seated figurines of the goddess Isis suckling the infant Horus; hippopotami; and recumbent lions. Amulet types that were restricted to Levels I and IIA are the god Min, falcons (Pl. XXVIII:11), the red and white crowns of Lower and Upper Egypt, and rams—shown as both recumbent animals (Pl. XXVIII:12) and striding anthropomorphic gods. The relative scarcity of ram amulets, only six of which were found, is curious given the fact that the local deity was Banebdjed, the ram.

Pl. XXVIII:11   7M50. Square V, Locus 13, Level IIB. Falcon amulet: green glazed faience; suspension loop on back. H=2.40 cm.

Pl. XXVIII:12   7M32. Square II, Locus 4, Level IIA. Recumbent ram amulet: light blue glazed faience; suspension loop on back. L=1.70 cm.

Pl. XXVIII:13   7M3. Square I, Locus 1, Level IIB. Thoth amulet: light blue glazed faience; striated cylindrical suspension loop on top of head. H=2.40 cm.

Fragments of faience vessels, mostly of unidentifiable form, were common in all levels. Small, globular vessels (Pl. XXX:1) and flat based cups with slightly flaring sides and everted rims (Pl. XXX:2) may have been the two most prevalent types. Some two dozen fragments of New Year's vessels—a reconstructed version of which is shown on Pl. XXX:3—came from Levels I-II.

5. Various Finds

Pl. XXX:1   Uncatalogued. Square V, Locus 43, Level IIC. Faience vessel rim, no traces of glaze. Rim diameter = 7.40 cm.

Pl. XXX:2   7M137. Square V, Locus 40, Level IIA. Blue glazed faience cup. H=4.30 cm.

Pl. XXX:3   Reconstruction of New Year's vessel. Rim and neck: 8M67 (Square IX, Locus 67, Level I). Body form and design based on numerous fragments. Inscription: wpt rnpt nfr: "Happy New Year" found on a number of pieces—e.g. 7M124 (Square V, Locus 33, Level IID), 7MI18 (Square V, Locus 43, Level IIC), 8MI7 (Square X, surface).

Scarabs (Pl. XXXI:1-3)

Fourteen scarabs were found during the two seasons. Five were made of faience, five of steatite, and four of ivory. They included two commemorative scarabs of Tuthmosis III from Level I and two Ramesside scarabs from Level IIC.

Pl. XXXI:1   7M43. Square III, Locus 26, Level IIA. Faience scarab amulet, no traces of glaze; pierced lengthwise for suspension. Inscription: mʒj nb rꜥ (?): "lion of Re" (?) or "Re is lord" (?). Possibly Psamtik I. L=0.65 cm.

Comparative material: W.M. Flinders Petrie, *Scarabs and Cylinders with Names* (British School of Archaeology in Egypt and Egyptian Research Account. Twenty-first Year, 1915) (London: School of Archaeology in Egypt, 1917), pl. 55:6; Erik Hornung, et al., *Skarabäen und andere Siegelamulette aus Basler Sammlungen* (Ägyptische Denkmäler in der Schweiz. Band 1) (Mainz: Philipp van Zabern, 1976), B31 (p. 378). [James P. Allen]

Pl. XXXI:2   7M104. Square III, Locus 44, Level IIA. White stone scarab amulet, pierced lengthwise for suspension. Inscription: zʒ rꜥ : "Son of Re." L=0.50 cm.

Comparative material: Hornung, *Skarabäen*, B41 (p. 380); Percy E. Newberry, *Scarabs* (University of Liverpool Institute of Archaeology, Egyptian Antiquities) (London: Archibald Constable and Co. Ltd., 1908), pl. 41:23. [James P. Allen]

Pl. XXXI:3   8M84. Square IX, Level IIC. Fragment of steatite scarab amulet, underside sheared off from main body and preserved; upper part of cartouche with prenomen of Ramesses II in upper field; king shown smiting captive with hands raised in supplication before Amun. H=1.40 cm.

Comparative material: W.C. Hayes, *The Scepter of Egypt. A Background for the Study of the Egyptian Antiquities in The Metropolitan*

Museum of Art, Part II (New York: Harper in cooperation with the Metropolitan Museum of Art, 1953), p. 345, fig. 217, bottom row, second from right, MMA No. 26.7230. [James P. Allen]

Terracotta amulet moulds (Pl. XXXII:1-5)

Some two dozen terracotta moulds for casting faience amulets were found in Levels I-II. The majority came from Level IIA and the Level IIC sherd layer. Most of the moulds have the shape of a flattened hemisphere or irregular disk, which fits neatly into the palm of the hand. The impression of the amulet is set into the flatter side of the mould and has a shallower depression extending out to the edge of the mould on either side—presumably to hold the rod-shaped object that created the suspension hole. Moulds for single and multiple *udjat* amulets (Pl. XXXII:1, 4) were the only two types found that exactly matched excavated amulets. Moulds for which corresponding amulet types were not found include large Bes heads (Pl. XXXII:2); Pan heads (Pl. XXXII:3); Bes heads with broad collars; a Sakhmet head with sun disk, *uraeus*, and broad collar; a small but extremely detailed Bes figure; and a bovine (Pl. XXXII:5) and a feline head.

Pl. XXXII:1   7M134a. Square V, Locus 15, Level IIA. Terracotta mould for multiple *udjat* amulet. Maximum diameter = 3.80 cm., Th. = 1.80 cm.

Pl. XXXII:2   7M122. Square V, Locus 43, Level IIC. Terracotta mould for Bes head amulet. Maximum diameter = 8.30 cm., Th. = 3.90 cm.

Pl. XXXII:3   7M126. Square V, Locus 15, Level IIA. Terracotta mould for Pan head amulet. Maximum diameter = 4.10 cm., Th. = 1.95 cm.

Pl. XXXII:4   7M107. Square I, Locus 1, Level IIB. Terracotta mould for *udjat* amulet. Maximum diameter = 5.30 cm., Th. = 1.80 cm.

Pl. XXXII:5   7M63. Square III, Locus 26, Level IIA. Terracotta mould for bovine head amulet. Maximum diameter = 3.20 cm., Th. = 1.50 cm.

Terracotta ram figurines (Pl. XXXIII:1-4)

Ten terracotta heads of the type illustrated on Pl. XXXIII were found during the two seasons. Although a number of examples (e.g. Pl. XXXIII:3-4) resemble a rooster or hoopoe with a flaring crest, rudimentary beak, and large eyes, others preserve traces of shoulders or haunches (Pl. XXXIII:1), and one piece was attached to the front of a quadruped body. These figurines, which appear to be unique to Mendes, seem to represent rams with a sun disk or plumed crest on the head. All the pieces once had horizontally projecting horns of unknown length, which have broken off and left only a crude stump on each side of the head.

Pl. XXXIII:1   7M114. Square VI, Locus 41, Level IIB. Terracotta ram figurine head, broken just below shoulders or haunches; traces of white slip. H=5.00 cm.

Pl. XXXIII:2   7M72. Square II, Locus 4, Level IIA. Terracotta ram figurine head, broken at neck. H=5.20 cm.

Pl. XXXIII:3   7M51. Square I, Locus 1, Level IIB. Terracotta ram figurine head, broken at neck. H=7.00 cm.

Pl. XXXIII:4   7M155. Square II, Locus 26, Level IIB. Terracotta ram figurine head, broken at neck. H=7.75 cm.

"Tokens" (Pl. XXXIV:1)

By far the most common objects found in the course of the excavations were pot sherds that had been re-worked into crude discs. A group of these "tokens" that were found together in a jar in Square II, Locus 4, Level IIA, along with an egg-shaped quartzite grinder, two conical pieces of limestone, and three small juglets, are illustrated on Pl. XXXIV:1. These "tokens" are frequently found in Late Period contexts (personal communication from other excavators including Richard Fazzini, John Holladay, Jr., and Jean Yoyotte) and are commonly called—and dismissed as—gaming pieces. However, their frequency at Mendes—some 536 of pottery and seven of stone—suggests a more practical function. Unfortunately, statistical analyses of the tokens by locus, level, size, material, and even weight has failed to reveal any patterns that might elucidate that function.

For loci in Levels I-IID, the proportion of the number of tokens found to the amount of pottery excavated (a more valid statistic than simple numbers of tokens, given differing amounts of deposition among loci) is consistent; the proportion is significantly lower for Level III. Most tokens have diameters between 3.0 and 4.5 cm., but sizes vary all the way from less than 1.0 cm. to as much as 9.0 cm. Token weights do not cluster in incremental groups that would indicate that the objects served as weights. Tokens are made from sherds of every fabric; the relative proportion of fabrics among tokens and all excavated sherds are the same. There was even one Attic black figure token.

Mitannian cylinder seal (Pl. XXXIV:2-3)

A small steatite cylinder seal, self-glazed by heating before it was carved, was found in the Level IID debris in Square VII. The cylinder belongs to the Common Style of Mitannian glyptic as defined by Edith Porada in *Seal Impressions of Nuzi* (The Annual of the American Schools of Oriental Research Vol. XXIV for 1944-1945), pp. 12-13. The piece is almost certainly contemporary with the tablets and associated seal impressions of the time of Teḫiptilla at Nuzi, which would give it a date early in the second half of the 15th century B.C.

(*Ibid.*, p. 11). In style and composition, the cylinder is closest to those of Porada's Group III (pp. 17-22), although it lacks the "bouquet-tree" common to most of that group.

    Pl. XXXIV:2-3 8M80. Square VII, Level IID. Mitannian cylinder seal: white steatite, self-glazed by heating before carving; pierced vertically by two drill holes which meet in center. H=2.45 cm., Diameter = 1.10 cm.

CHAPTER 6

A THIRD INTERMEDIATE PERIOD RELIEF FRAGMENT

Victoria L. Solia

A soft white limestone fragment with a partially preserved divine representation was found during the 1979 season in a pit dug into the Level III dumped debris. The piece (Pl. XXXV) is described here separately as a relief of some artistic merit, with certain peculiarities of style, which may be attributed to the Third Intermediate Period.

The fragment has clear fractures only along the left and bottom edges. The rough, though probably worked, upper and right edges and rear surface suggest that the god's image was cut out from a larger monument for re-use in antiquity.

The representation of a god's head in left profile is executed in low raised relief. The long, squarish face of the god, with its somewhat vapid expression, is defined by the bordering lines of the accoutrements. These consist of a plain tripartite wig with tab and beardstrap. The wig rests low upon the forehead, and the forepart of the wig rises quite steeply, in a line nearly perpendicular to the upper edge of the fragment. Any identifying emblem that might have existed above the wig would have been lost when the slab was re-cut. The tab is short and carved in one with the wig. The lower foreportion of the wig, perhaps a lappet, hangs directly below the tip of the earlobe and almost entirely frames the ear. The ear, with well articulated helix, is positioned at a level approximately between eyebrow and nostril. No parallel has yet been found for the pronounced, unnatural manner in which the tragus is inverted. Due to surface damage at the tip of the lobe, it is not possible to determine if the ear was nicked. The beardstrap, indicated by two incised lines, marks the contour of the jawline and disappears under the tab. The tip of the chin and beard are broken away. The front of the neck is also missing; but the ends of two parallel wrinkle lines are preserved.

In contrast to the flat wig and face area, the individual features are formed by incised lines and a minimum of modelling. The eye is slightly tilted in relation to the contour of the wig below the ear. Its deepest carved point is at the inner canthus. The upper eyelid rim is outlined and continues into the cosmetic line. The straight eyebrow, also formed by two incised lines, dips above the outer canthus and parallels the cosmetic line. The nose is long and slightly aquiline above the blunted tip; a small nostril is indicated. The firm mouth is set close to the tip of the nose, the corner is slightly drawn back, and the lips are straight.

The present state of the relief, without inscriptions or identifying emblems, does not permit the identification of a specific god. The dating of the fragment is difficult given the uniformity of style and image employed by the ancient Egyptians in their representations of the deity and the secondary context in which the piece was found. The calm and bland pleasantness of expression in the representation seems to evoke a New Kingdom ideal of beauty. However, the relief is removed from the New Kingdom by a length of time during which the continuous rendering of earlier prototypes has produced a standard, somewhat formal genre. Due to these factors, and the fact that carving in raised relief was revived during Dynasty XXII, a tentative attribution to Dynasty XXII or shortly thereafter is here suggested on stylistic grounds.

Pl. XXXV: 7M95. Square I, Locus 43, pit dug into Level III. Limestome relief fragment. H=9.4 cm., W=7.2 cm., Th.=2.2 cm.

CHAPTER 7

CONCLUSIONS

Karen L. Wilson

The past two seasons' work at Mendes have yielded new information concerning several aspects of the ancient town during the Third Intermediate and Late Period. The results also shed light on material previously excavated at a number of major Delta sites and provide for a new interpretation of that material. It is perhaps most logical to discuss these disparate ramifications of the excavations on a level-by-level basis, following the history of the area beginning with the earliest stratum reached in 1980.

Levels V, IV, and III constitute a series of three purposeful fill strata. The pottery and small finds that they yielded are homogeneous in type and range in date from the Ramesside to the Third Intermediate Period, with no apparent chronological development from level to level. These strata are part of a land fill or construction operation of almost staggering proportions, the purpose of which remains a matter of conjecture. The debris was exposed to a maximum thickness of six meters, but the bottom was not reached. The ridge that these strata comprise extends to the northwest toward the sacred precinct for almost 150 meters, and its weathered north edge reveals loose, pink-gray Level III deposit for that entire distance. Both this homogeneity of Level III over a considerable area and the nature of Level IV—lumps of nearly pure clay, packed in a layer of uniform thickness with smooth upper and lower surfaces—attest to the purposeful nature of these fills and the amount of planning and labor that went into the completion of the project.

The date of the depositing, however, is somewhat problematical. Although the latest artifacts in the fill are of Third Intermediate Period date, they provide only a *terminus post quem* for the strata. At the end of Level III, the top surface of this artificial mound was not horizontal, but sloped down toward the south within the area excavated. A level surface over the area was created by the subsequent Levels IID and IIC. Level IID contained mixed Third Intermediate and Late Period material, whereas Level IIC was completely Dynasty XXVI in date. Because these later two levels appear to be purposeful fills similar in intent to Levels V-III, it seems reasonable to suggest that all five strata were deposited as part of a single operation. Levels V-III, therefore, would consist of Third Intermediate Period occupation debris that was used as fill some time during Dynasty XXVI. The quantity of material that was available for such a project confirms the historical evidence for the importance of Mendes during the Third Intermediate Period.

The reason for the filling operation is unknown and may remain enigmatic because of the destruction of the north edge of the ridge by the Late Hellenistic foundation system. It is tempting to suggest that the ridge was built as the southern edge of the so-called harbor, just as the precinct enclosure wall served as the western edge, and that it was designed to provide high, dry land for a series of buildings of some commercial importance. The badly destroyed remains of Levels IIB and IIA, however, do not go far toward supporting such an hypothesis, although the foundations of Level I attest to the subsequent existence of a large complex or complexes of buildings on the site.

Although the artifacts from Levels V-IID come from a secondary context, they provide the first excavated evidence, however scanty, for the material culture of Mendes during the Third Intermediate Period. The predominant ceramic ware is a hard, dense, well levigated and well fired alluvial clay, which is worked in a limited repertoire of forms: primarily deep bowls and cups, widemouthed jars with folded over or thickened rims, and high vertical necked jars. The use of cream colored slips, applied uniformly or as streaky white washes, characterizes these wares. The presence of Mycenaean sherds and a Mitannian cylinder seal attest to the site's contacts—either direct or through an intermediary or intermediaries—with other areas in the eastern Mediterranean basin. The differences in artifactual assemblages between these levels and those above may have chronological, or simple functional, bases. Faience is almost completely absent, whereas flint blades and flakes and metal implements are relatively common.

With Level IIC, there is a marked change in assemblages of artifacts, which remain relatively constant through Level I. The repeated cutting down of later levels into earlier strata may be in part responsible for this artifactual continuity. However, the absence of noticeable variation must also attest to the fact that relatively little time elapsed during the accumulation of these strata. The largest single category of finds in these later levels is faience amulets. Careful analysis of the wide variety of types and their proveniences may eventually reveal level-by-level changes in form and frequency of these types, but such differences are not readily apparent at this time. Also characteristic of the artifactual assemblages of Levels IIC-I were fragments of faience vessels, scarabs, terracotta moulds (most of them from Level IIA), terracotta figurines, and the ubiquitous pottery "tokens."

The ceramic assemblage of Levels IIC-I was recognizable at a glance from that of Levels V-IID. The repertoire of forms was greater, as was the range in fabric types—from coarse, straw tempered, hand made wares through well levigated, organic tempered Nile clay wares, with an admixture of marl clay sherds with a pinkish or greenish color. Computer analyses of the ceramic data will reveal the spatial and temporal variations in these types—variations that were not immediately discernable in the field.

Over much of the excavated area, Level IIC was sealed by a thin deposit of nearly solid sherds. East Greek pottery from this layer ranged in date from 615 to 580/560 B.C., providing a *terminus post quem* for the level. The fact that a North Ionian sherd from Level IID (Pl. XXIII:1) is also datable between 580 and 560 B.C. supports the theory that these two fill layers were deposited at a single time—probably during the third quarter of the sixth century B.C. If the entire filling operation occurred at a single time, as suggested above, it therefore probably dates to the reign of King Amasis and is contemporary with that monarch's rebuilding of the sanctuary. Unfortunately, the chronological range of the succeeding levels is as yet impossible to determine with certainty. Clazomenian sherds from Levels IIA and I (Pl. XXV:1-2) provide a *terminus post quem* of 550-540 B.C. for those levels and may allow us to suggest that they all pre-date the Persian conquest of 525 B.C. Although the amount of accumulation comprising Levels IIB-I would seem to

7. Conclusions

suggest a somewhat longer time span, the strong continuity in ceramic and other artifactual types may be taken to support a late Twenty-sixth Dynasty date for the three levels.

Level IIB was so badly destroyed by later cuts that nothing can be said concerning its original nature and function. The area was subsequently covered with large vats and burning pits apparently belonging to an industrial quarter where faience objects were produced (Level IIA). At this stage in its history, the area closely resembles the deposits which built up above the Ptah temple constructed by Ramesses II at Mit Rahineh.[1] The type of occupation, and the pottery and other artifacts from the two sites are nearly identical[2] and indicate an identity of function for the two areas. The Mit Rahineh material was dated primarily to the Third Intermediate Period by the excavators. In light of the close parallels with a level at Mendes which cannot possibly be earlier than the second half of the sixth century B.C., however, the date of the Mit Rahineh deposits needs to be reexamined.

The building complexes of Level I belong to a Late Period architectural type that has yet to be properly defined and discussed, even though examples have been excavated at a number of Delta sites. A detailed study of these complexes is being prepared for separate publication, and only a brief overview will be presented here.

The three structures most similar to the one at Mendes were excavated by Petrie at Memphis, Naukratis, and Tell Defenneh. Petrie published only verbal descriptions, a crude plan, and a photograph of the building at Memphis.[3] He first called the structure, which was situated north of the Ptah temple, a fort, but he later changed the designation to the Palace of Apries, based on the discovery of a limestone column bearing the cartouche of that king. The description of the building and the photograph suggest the presence of a structure or structures similar to Building D. The walls averaged fourteen feet thick and "much of the north end had been successively extended by building up a cellular substructure of brick shafts domed over." Walls of what Petrie saw as an earlier palace had bricks laid on a concave bed and were reinforced with wooden beams.

In 1976, Kemp spent two and a half days studying the palace and published a detailed account of his observations.[4] He noted that the building belonged to a single constructional phase and that all the major vertical walls descended all the way down through the mound. Rows of beam holes were visible in these walls below the floor level. The spaces between the walls were packed with earthy rubble which had all the appearance of deliberate fill and was capped by a thin layer of mud bruck over which the limestone floor was laid.

---

[1] Rudolf Anthes, et al., *Mit Rahineh 1956* (Museum Monographs) (Philadelphia: The University Museum, 1965), pp. 20-30.

[2] *Ibid.*, No. 94-122 (stone pounders and other tools), 176-183 (flints), 184-241 (amulets), 225-236 (faience vessel fragments), 242-249 (terracotta figurines), 258-294 (terracotta amulet moulds), 295-303 (spools), 304-306 (pump drill handles), 329-341 (*udjats*), 359-387 (finger rings) and most of the pottery types illustrated on pl. 56-68.

[3] W.M. Flinders Petrie, *Memphis I* (British School of Archaeology in Egypt and Egyptian Research Account, 14th Year, 1908) (London: School of Archaeology in Egypt, University College and Bernard Quaritch, 1909), p. 4, pl. 1; *The Palace of Apries (Memphis II)* (British School of Archaeology in Egypt and Egyptian Research Account, 15th Year, 1909) (London: School of Archaeology in Egypt, University College and Bernard Quaritch, 1909), pp. 1-2, pl. 13 lower right.

[4] Barry J. Kemp, "The Palace of Apries at Memphis," *Mitteilungen des Deutschen Archäologischen Instituts Abteilung Kairo* 33 (1977), pp. 101-108.

7. Conclusions

The northernmost section consisted of brick cells, oval in plan, which were probably originally domed and seem to have been filled with rubble only to half their height.

Kemp appears to have accepted Petrie's statement that the palace was an above ground platform designed to support a superstructure of columned halls and rooms, whose floors stood at a height of over 13 meters above the surrounding countryside. It is, however, possible that the "fosse" along the south facade of the building is actually a foundation trench, which Petrie noticed only on this side of the building because it abutted on a second structure to the south. The palace platform, analogous in so many details to Building D at Mendes, would make more structural sense as a subterranean foundation than as a free standing terrace, and its remains need to be reexamined with this question in mind.

"The Great Mound" at Naukratis is the second building of this type excavated by Petrie.[5] It was a square measuring 180 feet on a side and contained numerous chambers both square and rectangular in form. Its walls, like those of Building D, had a pronounced inward batter, and the courses bowed up toward the corners. Petrie also interpreted "The Great Mound" as an above ground defensive structure—a fort—and noted that the "cells" were only accessible from the top, which was seventeen feet above ground. The building appears from the plan to have been closely surrounded by a wall, similar to the "enclosure wall" on the north and east of Building D. Probably more of the superstructure of "The Great Mound" was preserved than of Building D. The cells above the domes communicated by stone-lined doorways, and each was surrounded by two ledges, one above the other, which Petrie suggests may have supported plank floors.

The closest parallel for the Level I complex—in terms not only of architecture but also of pottery and small finds—was excavated at Tell Defenneh.[6] Although the exact stratigraphic relationships of the various structures published by Petrie on the plan is unclear, the individual elements are the same as Level I at Mendes. A large square building measuring approximately 145 feet on a side was preserved to a height of 24 feet above the base. Several of the numerous interior chambers preserved the bases of the springing of domes. The building was surrounded by a narrow ditch which Petrie interpreted as a type of dry moat, but which is more likely to have been the foundation trench for the structure. Under the four corners of the building were foundation deposits of Psamtik I.

To the north of the building was a solid mud brick platform (possibly comparable to Buildings B and C) and, to the north and east, other complexes with doorless chambers, probably similarly domed (compare Building A). Several rooms to the southeast of the square building contained quantities of East Greek pottery mixed with jar sealings of Psamtik II and Amasis. This East Greek pottery is similar to that found at Mendes, and the rest of the ceramic corpus is nearly identical to that from Levels I-II.

The building complex of Level I at Mendes, therefore, can be seen as one of a number of similar complexes constructed at various Delta sites during the Late Period. The function of these structures has not yet been determined satisfactorily. Petrie suggested that the domed chambers were used for storage but, because he interpreted the buildings as above

---

[5] W.M. Flinders Petrie, et al., *Naukratis. Part I. 1884-5* (Third Memoir of the Egypt Exploration Fund) (London: Trübner and Co., 1886), pp. 24-26, pl. 42-43.

[6] W.M. Flinders Petrie, et al., *Tanis. Part II. Nebesheh (Am) and Defenneh (Tahpanhes)* (Fourth Memoir of the Egypt Exploration Fund) (London: Trübner and Co., 1888), pp. 52-80, pl. 24-45.

7. Conclusions

ground structures rather than foundations, he saw their main purpose to be defensive. Further excavation of Building D at Mendes, including clearing of all the chambers to the bottom, and analyses of samples taken from those chambers, should begin to elucidate the function of these still enigmatic structures.

After Level I, this area of the mound appears to have been unoccupied for several centuries. Its history picks up again during the Late Hellenistic period. A mud brick foundation system some 45 meters wide from north to south was sunk into the north edge of the ridge, but no later structures seem to have been built atop the Level I remains. The foundations seem to be more in the nature of a platform or terrace than of a true building foundation. The rubble filled chambers within the fabric of the brickwork suggest no coherent plan of overlying walls and rooms. The structure appears, from its contents, to be contemporary with the burials in Kom el-'Izam, which lies across the harbor depression to the north.[7] Aerial photographs reveal that that mound was enclosed by a wall,[8] and it may also have had the character of a terrace or platform. Although the exact nature, purpose, or function of these structures has not yet been determined, their existence attests to continued interest in and activity at the ancient town of Mendes after the founding of the neighboring Hellenistic settlement of Thmuis.

---

[7] Two soundings have been made in this mound. The first was directed by Dr. Labib Habachi in April of 1947 (see Herman DeMeulenaere and Pierre MacKay, *Mendes II* (Warminster: Aris and Phillips Ltd., 1976), pp. 17-18); the second was undertaken during the fifth season of excavations at Mendes in 1977.

[8] Emma Swan Hall and Bernard V. Bothmer, eds., *Mendes I* (Cairo: American Research Center in Egypt, 1980), pl. 28.

PLATES

Plate I. The Naos, seen from the northwest at the end of the 1966 excavation season.

Plate II   **Master survey plan of Mendes**

A. Naos

B. Old Kingdom limestone tombs

C. Old Kingdom mastabas, Old Kingdom and First Intermediate Period houses

D. Third Intermediate Period houses, excavated in 1964; possible location of temple bakeries

E. Granite sarcophagus in limestone casing, probably Twenty-ninth Dynasty in date

F. Site of 1977 excavation of sanctuary enclosure wall

G. Kom el-'Izam

H. Site of 1979-1980 excavations

I. Possible harbor of the ancient town

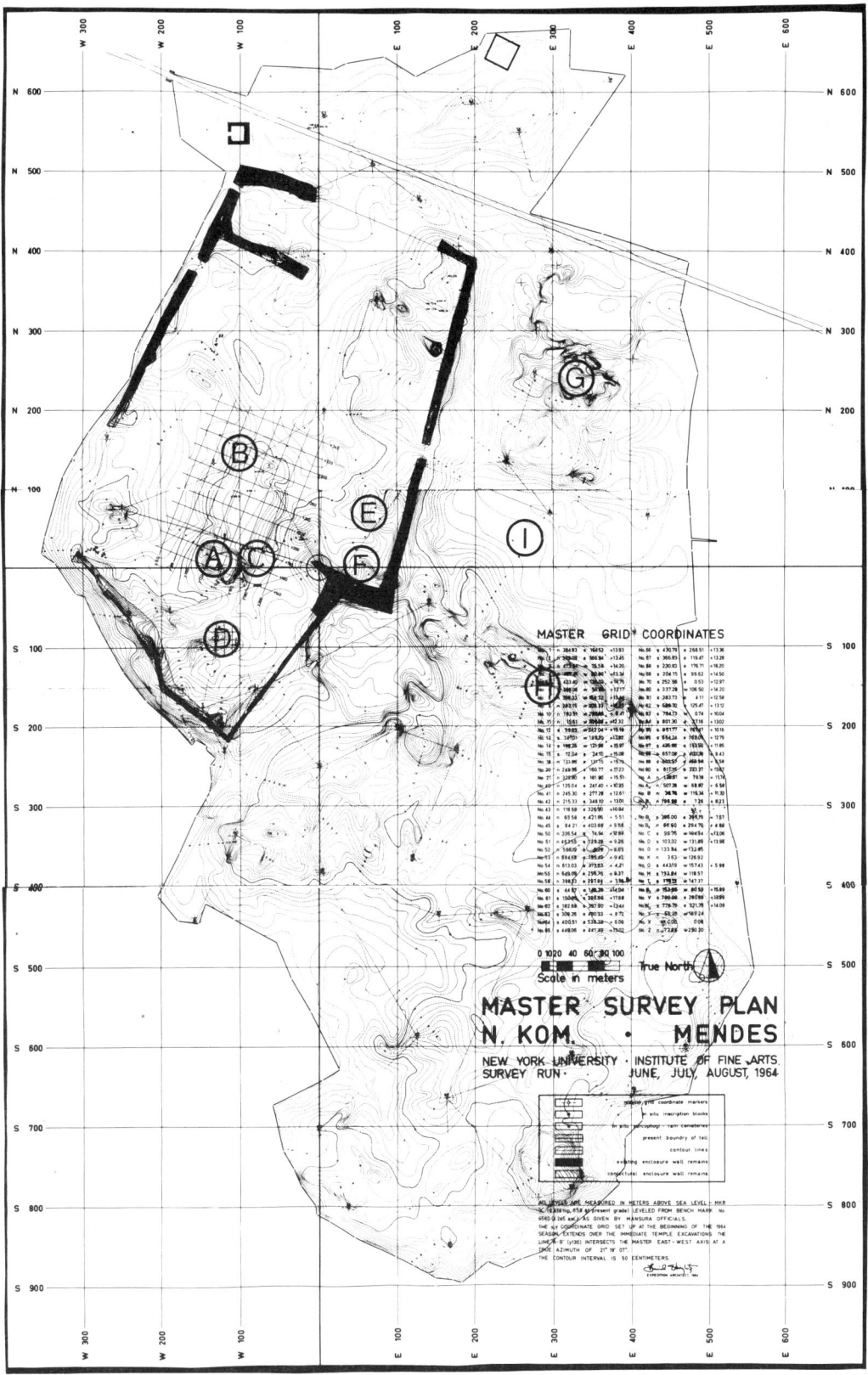

PLATE III

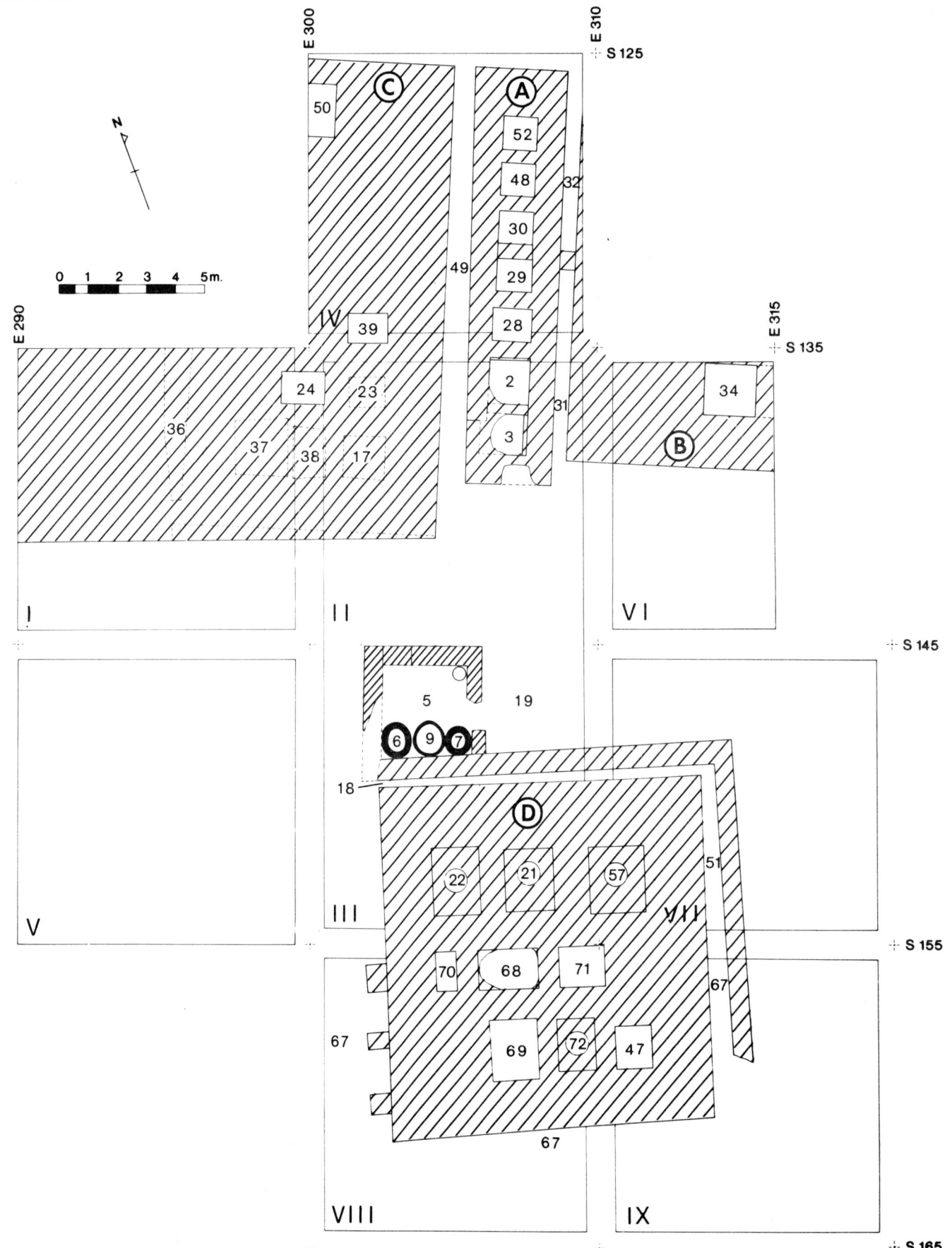

Plate III. Plan of Level I.

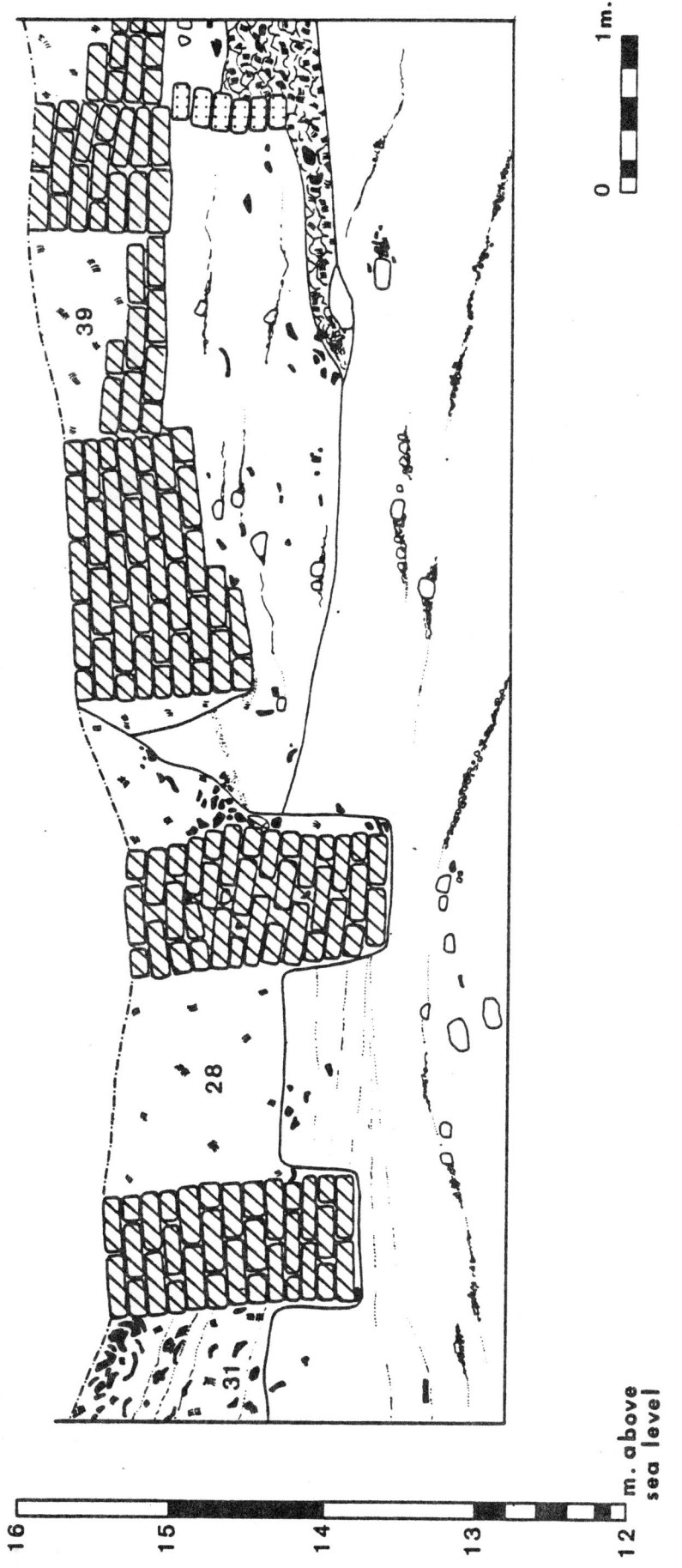

Plate IV. Square IV, South balk.

PLATE V

Plate V. Square II, Loci 3 and 2, looking southwest.

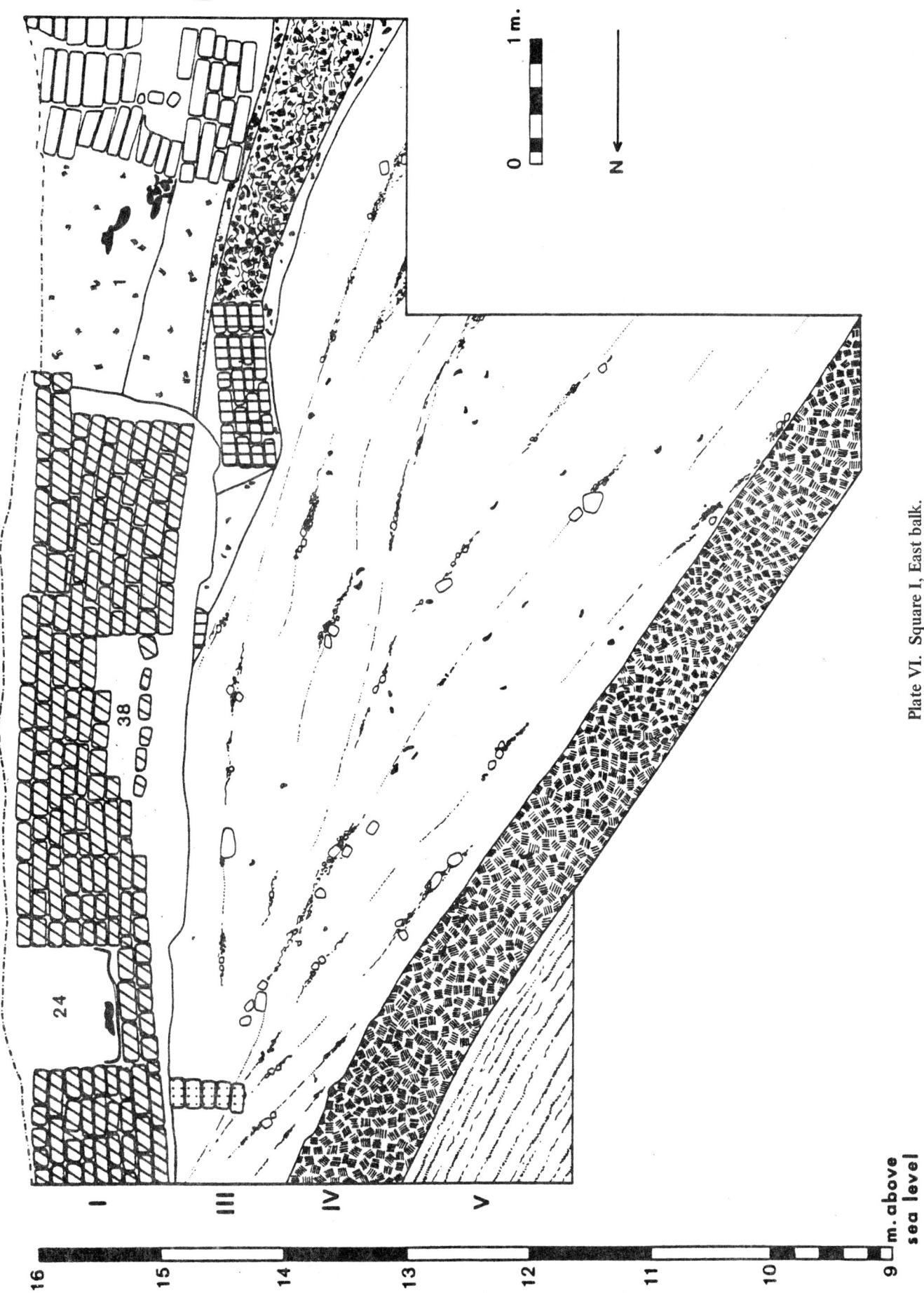

Plate VI. Square I, East balk.

PLATE VII

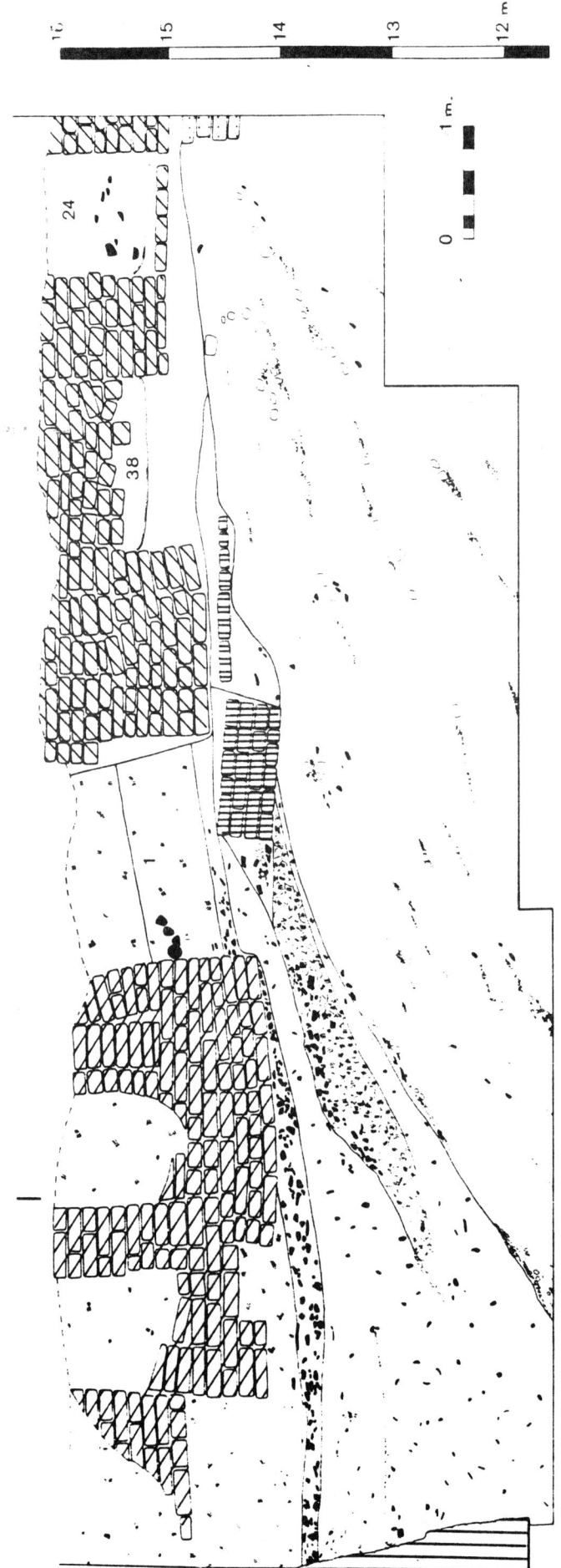

Plate VII. Square II and northern portion of Square III, West balk.

PLATE VIII

Plate VIII:1. Square III, Building D and Level IID wall, looking south.

Plate VIII:2. Square IX, Building D, looking northwest.

PLATE IX

Plate IX:2. Square VII, Building D, Locus 57, looking north.

Plate IX:1. Square VII, Building D and Level IID wall, looking southwest.

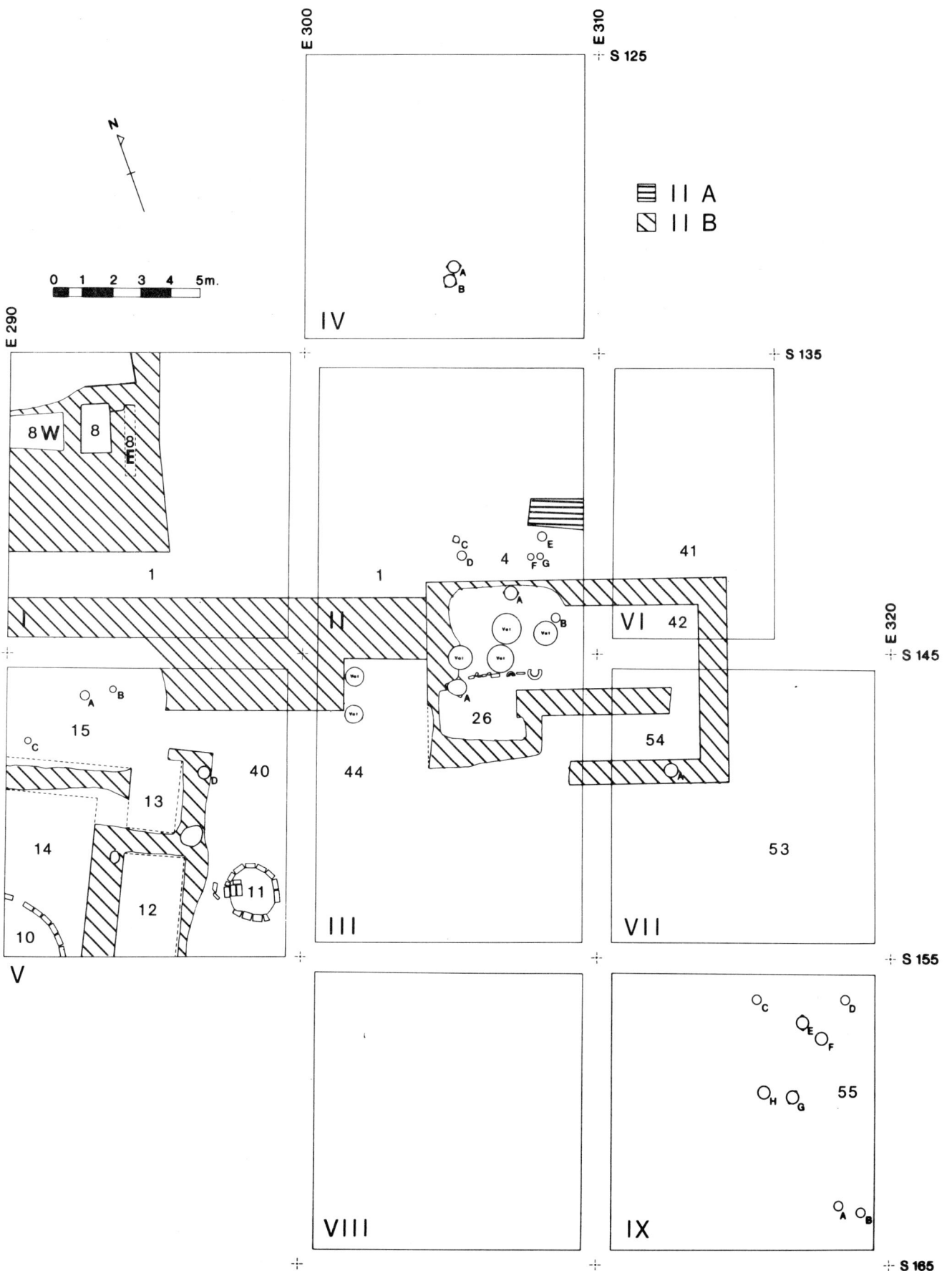

Plate X. Plan of Levels IIA and IIB.

PLATE XI

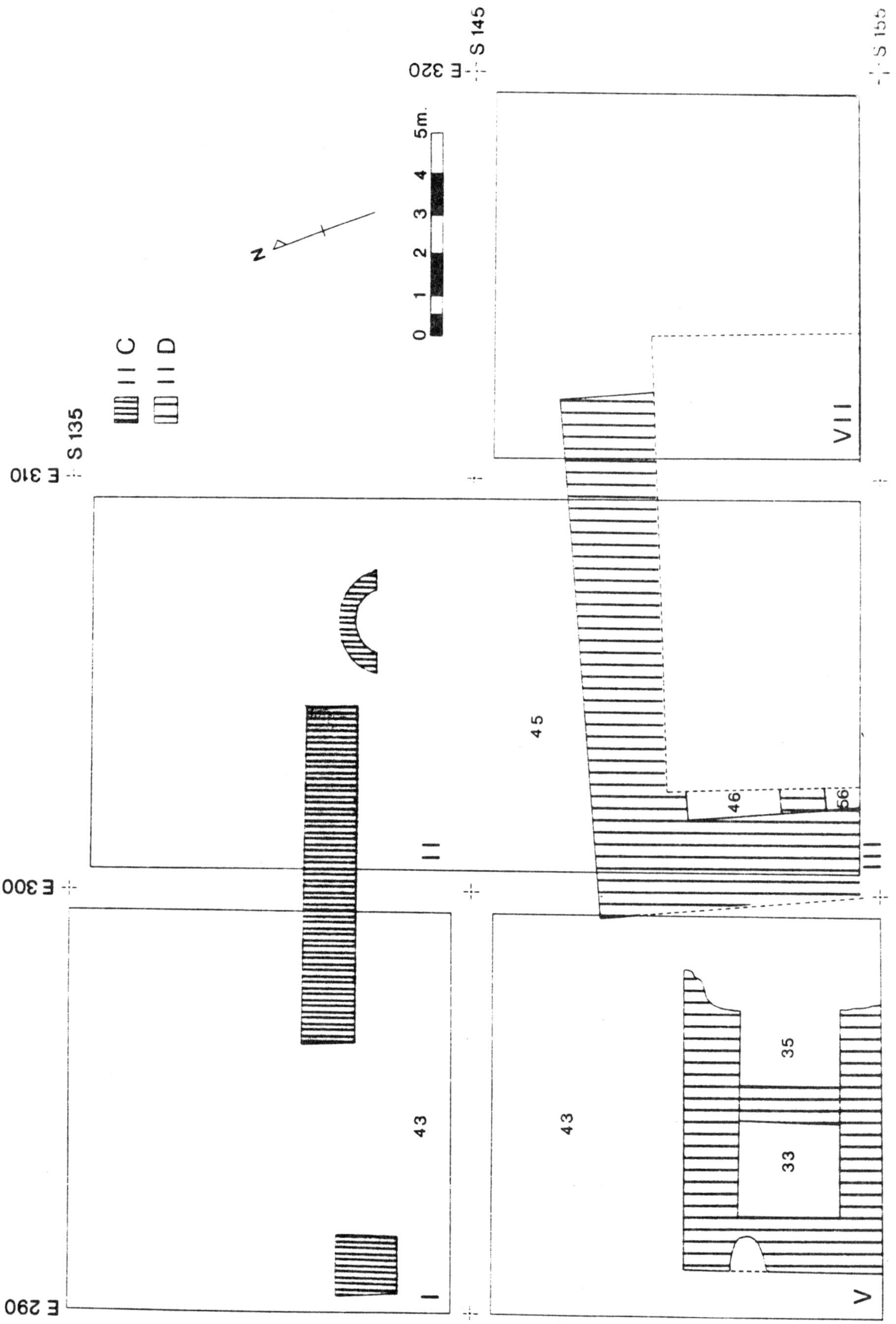

Plate XI. Plan of Levels IIC and IID.

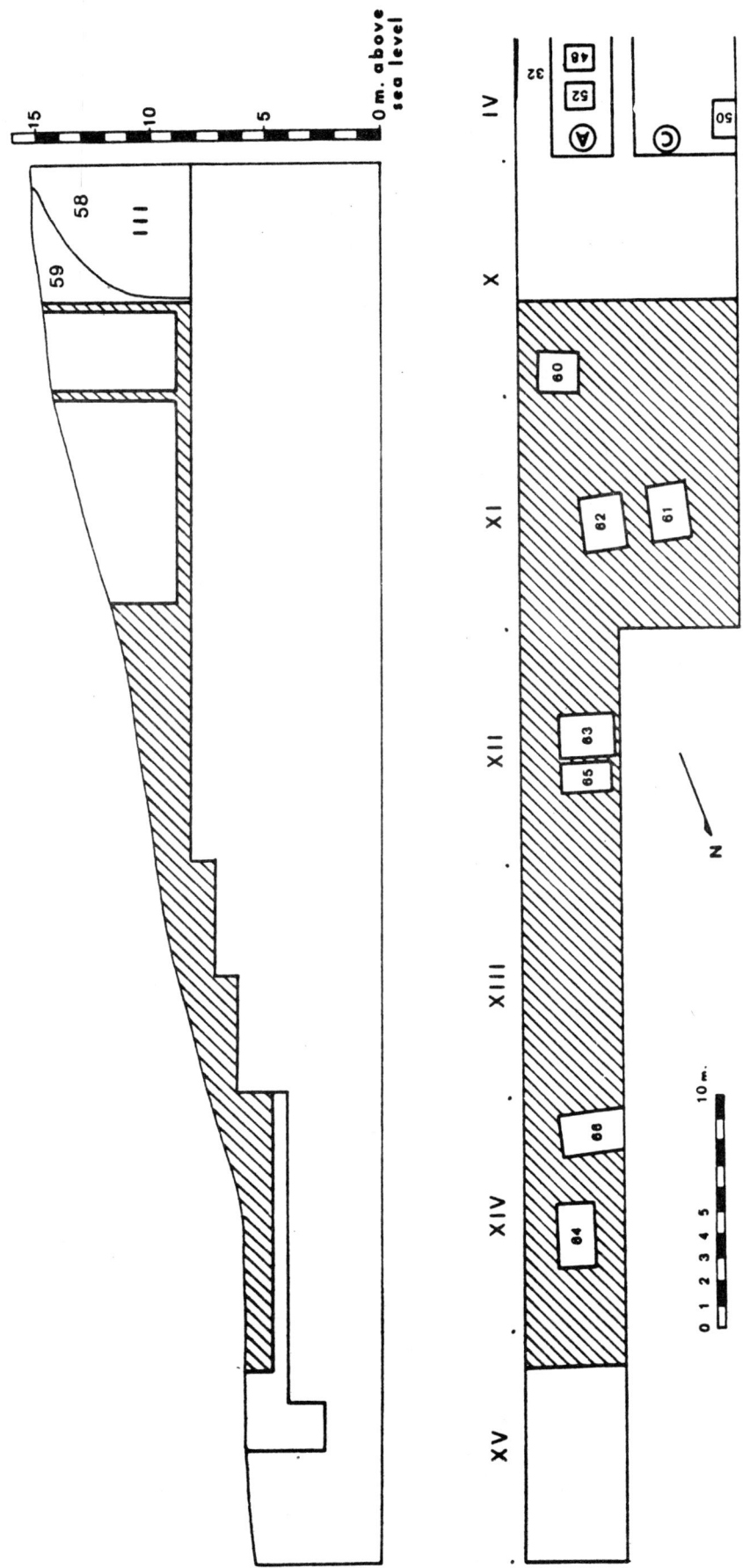

Plate XII. Squares X-XV, East balk (top) and plan (bottom).

PLATE XIII: Late Hellenistic Pottery Scale 1:4 (1-6) and 1:8 (7-9)

Type Number & Provenience	Description
1. 8MP165 Square X Surface	Bowl. Alluvial clay, grit temper, moderately fired. Surface: black (7.5YR 2.75/0), matte slip (?) interior and exterior. Wheel made. Incurving lip rim, ring base.
2. 8MP194 Square VII Surface	Small bowl. Alluvial clay, organic temper, well fired. Surface: red (10R 4/6), matte, wet smoothed. Wheel made. Flat, string cut base, carinated profile, modelled rim.
3. 8MP164 Square X Surface	Carinated bowl. Alluvial clay, grit temper, well fired. Surface: reddish brown, matte, wet smoothed exterior; red matte wash interior. Wheel made. Plain lip rim, ring base formed by cutting and scraping off excess clay.
4. 8MP142 Square X Locus 60	Cooking pot. Alluvial clay, grit temper, well fired. Surface: red (10R 5/8), thin matte slip exterior. Wheel made. Two horizontal loop handles flattened against body, interior rim trough and projection to take lid.
5. 8MP166 Square XIV Locus 64	Jug. Alluvial clay, organic temper, moderately fired. Surface: red (2.5YR 4/8), matte slip exterior and over rim. Wheel made. Modelled rim; stump of handle preserved on shoulder, upper attachment unknown; ring base.
6. 8MP150 Square X Surface	Jar. Alluvial clay, grit temper, well fired. Surface: white (2.5Y 8/2), matte slip exterior and interior. Wheel made. Plain lip rim, ring base with body projecting below bottom of ring.
7. 8MP226 Square XIV Locus 66	Widemouth jar. Alluvial clay, organic temper, moderately fired. Surface: red (10R 5/8), matte, wet smoothed. Wheel made. Modelled lip rim, flattened on top.
8. 8MP228 Square XI In Brickwork	Amphora base. Marl clay, grit temper, moderately fired. Surface: pink (7.5YR 7/4), matte, self slip. Wheel made.
9. 8MP229 Square XI Locus 61	Amphora base. Marl clay, grit temper, moderately fired. Surface: reddish yellow (5YR 6/6), matte self slip covered with smeary grayish wash (5YR 6/1) exterior. Wheel made. Knob base, hollow on interior.

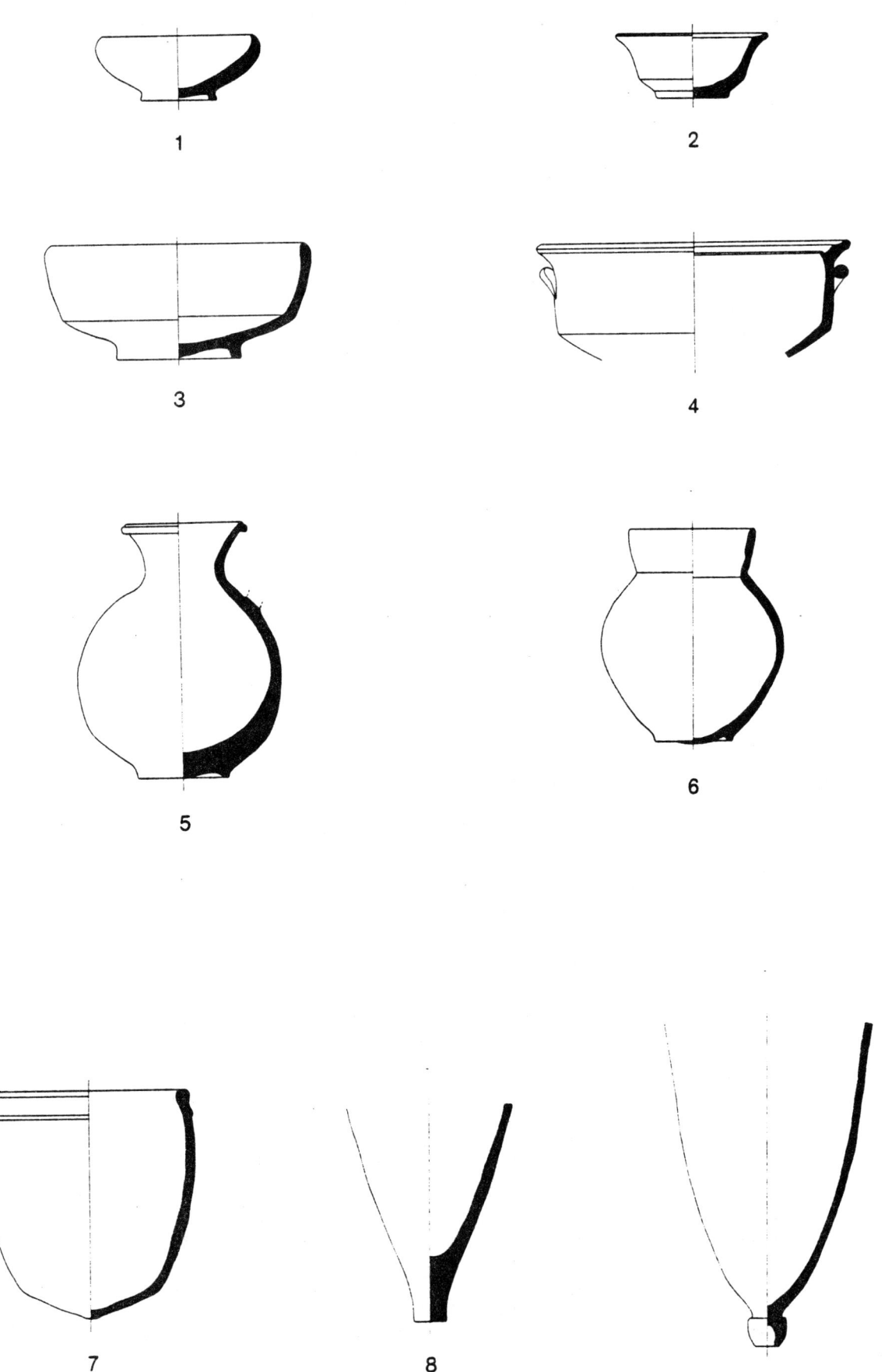

PLATE XIII

Plate XIV: Bowls   Scale 1:4

Type Number & Provenience	Description	Date
1. 7MP418 Square II Locus 1 Level IIB-C	Bowl. Greenish marl clay, organic and red grog temper, moderately fired. Surface: very pale brown (10YR 7/3), rough, matte. Wheel made. Flat string cut base and slightly modelled lip rim.	Late
2. 7MP543 Square I Level III	Bowl. Alluvial clay, organic temper. Lightly fired and soft, black core. Surface: reddish yellow (5YR 6/6), matte, probably rubbed over or scraped with reeds or some plant material, rough, pitted and scored. Hand made (?). Unmodelled direct rim.	Third Intermediate
3. 7MP673 Square V Locus 43 Level IID	Bowl. Alluvial clay, sand and straw temper. Fabric: red (10R 4/8). Surface: thick matte pink slip exterior (7.5YR 8/4), peeling. Probably hand made. Flat base, unmodelled direct rim.	Third Intermediate
4. 7MP581 Square IV Surface	Bowl. Alluvial clay, finely divided organic temper, well fired. Surface: red (2.5YR 5/8), matte, wet smoothed. Wheel made. Flat string cut base, unmodelled direct rim.	Ptolemaic (?)
5. 7MP619 Square V Locus 43 Level IIC	Bowl. Alluvial clay, organic temper, moderately fired. Surface: red (10R 5/8), matte, wet smoothed. Wheel made. Base uneven, with deep finger marks, unmodelled direct rim.	Late
6. 7MP20 Square V Level IIA	Carinated bowl. Alluvial clay, heavy organic temper, moderately fired, black core. Surface: red (10R 5/8), matte, wet smoothed, thin red wash (10R 4/8) interior. Wheel made. Flat string cut base, modelled direct rim.	Late
7. 7MP596 Square I Locus 1 Level IIB	Carinated bowl. Alluvial clay, organic temper, moderately fired. Surface: red (2.5YR 5/6), matte, wet smoothed. Wheel made. Unmodelled direct rim.	Late
8. 7MP13 Square I Locus 1 Level IIB	Carinated bowl. Alluvial clay, organic temper, moderately fired. Surface: red (10R 5/8), matte, wet smoothed. Wheel made. Flat string cut base, fabric or mat impressions on underside, modelled lip rim, ledge slanting upward.	Late
9. 7MP586 Square VI Locus 42 Level IIA	Carinated bowl. Alluvial clay, finely divided organic temper, moderately fired. Fabric: red (10R 5/8). Surface: red wash exterior (10R 4/8), slightly lustrous. Wheel made. Rounded base, 2 pierced lug handles, unmodelled direct rim, incised groove exterior.	Late
10. 7MP27 Square I Locus 1 Level IIB	Carinated bowl. Alluvial clay, finely divided organic temper. Surface: possible red wash (10R 5/8) exterior. Wheel made. Slightly rounded base scraped down on wheel, unmodelled direct rim with groove on exterior.	Late
11. 7MP316 Square I Locus 1 Level IIB	Carinated bowl. Alluvial clay, organic temper. Fabric: yellowish red (5YR 5/6), black core, moderately fired. Surface: red slip (10R 4/8) interior and exterior, matte. Wheel made. Slightly rounded base scraped down on wheel, unmodelled direct rim.	Late
12. 7MP388 Square I Level III	Bowl. Alluvial clay, finely divided organic temper and some sand, moderately fired, black core. Surface: reddish yellow (5YR 6/6), matte. Wheel made. Pointed base, blunted at tip, scraped down on wheel, modelled lip rim, rolled.	Third Intermediate
13. 7MP510 Square IV Level III	Bowl. Alluvial clay, finely divided organic temper, moderately fired. Surface: red (10R 5/8), matte, rough. Wheel made. Pointed base blunted at tip, scraped down on wheel, unmodelled direct rim.	Third Intermediate

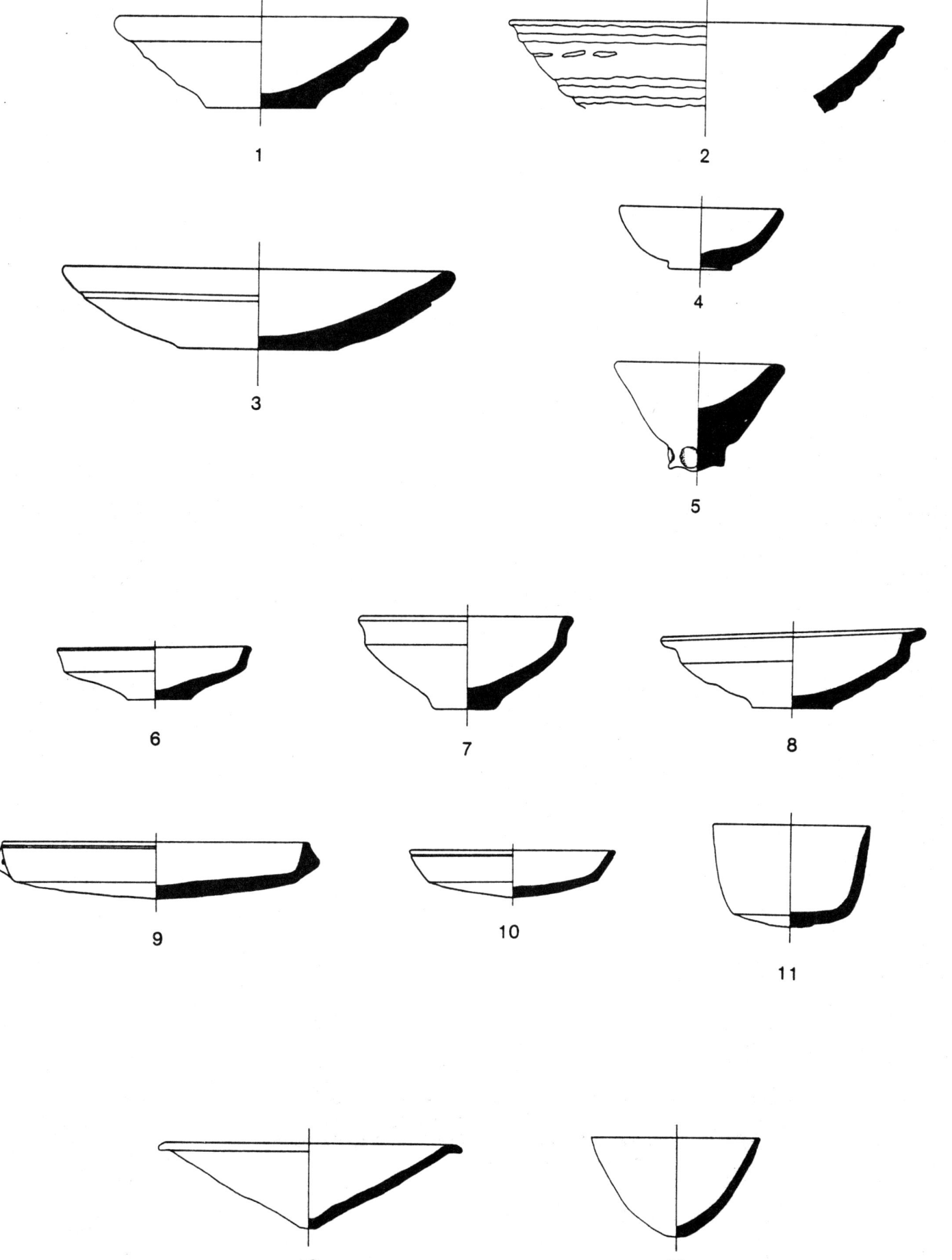

PLATE XIV

Plate XV: Lamp (1), Saucer (2), Chalices (3-4), Beakers (5-6), Basins (7-8), Trays (9-10) Scale: 1:4

Type Number & Provenience	Description	Date
1. 7MP32 Square I Locus 1 Level IIB	Lamp. Alluvial clay, organic temper, moderately fired. Surface: thick red slip (10R 4/8) interior (streak burnished) and exterior (matte). Rim blackened. Two triangles interior, incised after firing. Wheel made. Unmodelled direct rim.	Late
2. 7MP188 Square I Locus 1 Level IIB	Saucer. Alluvial clay, organic temper, moderately fired. Surface: red (10R 6/6), matte, wet smoothed. Wheel made. Uneven string cut base, unmodelled direct rim.	Late
3. 7MP102 Square III Locus 26 Level IIA	Chalice. Alluvial clay, organic temper, moderately fired. Surface: red (2.5YR 5/8), matte, wet smoothed. Wheel made. Thick string cut foot, unmodelled direct rim.	Late
4. 7MP410 Square V Locus 13 Level IIA-B	Chalice. Alluvial clay, organic temper, moderately fired. Surface: red (10R 5/8), matte, wet smoothed. Wheel made. Flat string cut foot, unmodelled direct rim.	Late
5. 7MP122 Square V Level IIA	Beaker. Alluvial clay, organic temper, moderately fired. Surface: red (10R 5/8), matte, wet smoothed. Wheel made. Hand finished, slightly pointed base, unmodelled direct rim.	Late
6. 7MP103 Square III Locus 26 Level IIA	Beaker. Alluvial clay, finely divided organic temper, moderately fired. Fabric: red (10R 5/8). Surface: red slip (10R 4/8) exterior, matte to slightly lustrous. Wheel made. Small bump in middle of base, unmodelled direct rim.	Late
7. 7MP71 Square III Locus 5 Level I	Basin. Alluvial clay, coarse organic temper, moderately fired, black core. Surface: red (10R 5/8), matte. Hand made. Modelled direct rim.	Late
8. 7MP508 Square II Locus 45 Level IIC	Basin. Alluvial clay, organic temper, moderately fired. Fabric: red (10R 5/8). Surface: reddish yellow (5YR 6/8), matte. Wheel made. Modelled lip rim, broadly flaring, interior projection.	Late
9. 7MP618 Square VI Locus 42 Level IIA	Tray. Alluvial clay, organic temper, moderately fired, black core. Surface: red (10R 5/8), matte, wet smoothed. Hand made, rim probably finished on tournette. Base broken, modelled lip rim, ledge slanting upward.	Late
10. 7MP149 Square VI Level III	Tray. Alluvial clay, coarse organic temper, moderately fired, red (10R 5/8) core. Surface: light reddish brown (5YR 6/4), matte, rough. Hand made. Slightly concave base, unmodelled direct rim.	Third Intermediate

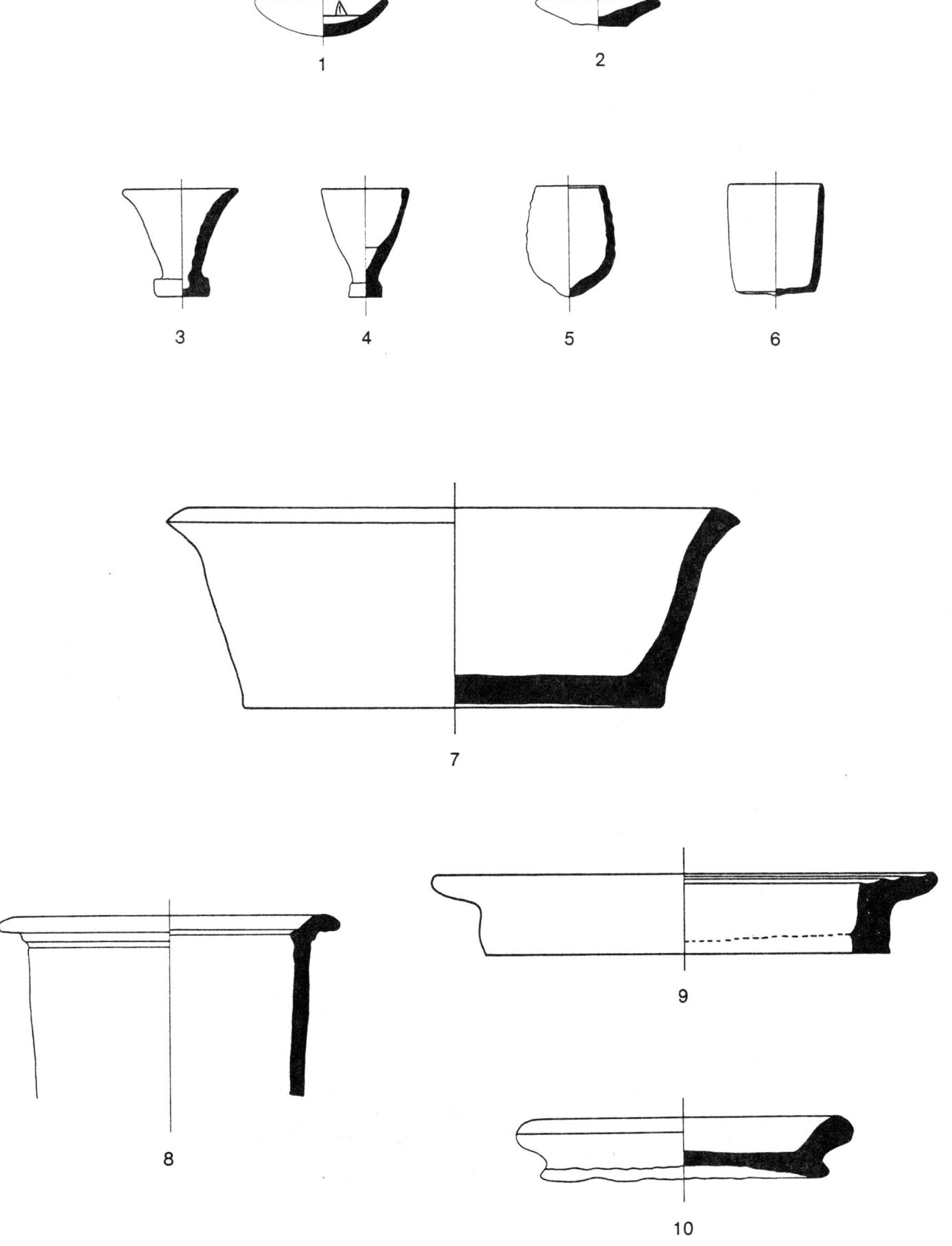

Plate XVI: Elongated jars (1-3), Globular jars (4-6), Small jars (7-9), Bes jar (10)   Scale 1:4

Type Number & Provenience	Description	Date
1. 7MP564 Square II Locus 4, Pot I Level IIA	Elongated jar. Alluvial clay, organic temper, moderately fired. Surface: red (10R 5/8), matte, wet smoothed. Wheel made, possibly in sections. Round base, slight nipple at tip, modelled lip rim, vessel asymmetrical.	Late
2. 7MP61 Square I Locus 1 Level IIB	Elongated jar. Alluvial clay, organic temper, moderately fired, dark core. Surface: red (10R 5/8), matte, wet smoothed. Wheel made. Round base, short vertical neck, unmodelled direct rim.	Late
3. 7MP94 Square I Locus 1 Level IIB	Elongated jar. Alluvial clay, organic temper, moderately fired. Surface: red (10R 5/8), matte, wet smoothed. Wheel made. Unmodelled direct rim, incised groove exterior.	Late
4. 7MP17 Square I Locus 24 Level I	Globular jar. Alluvial clay, organic temper, moderately fired. Fabric: yellowish red (5YR 5/6). Surface: red slip (10R 4/8) exterior, matte. Wheel made. Modelled neck and rim.	Late
5. 7MP81 Square I Locus 1 Level IIB	Jar neck. Alluvial clay, organic temper, moderately fired. Fabric: red (10R 5/8). Surface red slip (10R 4/8) exterior, streak burnished. Wheel made. Modelled lip rim, 2 raised ribs around neck.	Late
6. 7MP585 Square I Locus 43 Level IIC	Globular jar. Alluvial clay, organic temper, moderately fired. Surface: red wash (10R 5/8) exterior, matte. Wheel made. Sharply modelled neck and rim; incised lines around shoulder.	Late
7. 7MP48 Square I Locus 8 West Level IIB	Small jar. Alluvial clay, finely divided organic temper, moderately fired. Surface: red wash (10R 4/8) exterior, matte. Wheel made. Unmodelled direct rim.	Late
8. 7MP46 Square II Locus 4, in pot B Level IIA	Small jar. Alluvial clay, organic temper, moderately fired. Surface: red wash (10R 4/8) exterior, matte. Wheel made. Hand finished, slightly pointed base, modelled direct rim.	Late
9. 7MP434 Square V Locus 40 Level IIB	Small jar. Alluvial clay, organic temper, moderately fired. Surface: red (10R 5/8), matte, wet smoothed. Wheel made. Hand finished round base, unmodelled direct rim.	Late
10. 7MP186 Square V Locus 14 Level IIA-B	Bes jar. Alluvial clay, organic temper, moderately fired. Surface: red (10R 5/8), matte, wet smoothed. Wheel made. Modelled lip rim. Decorated with Bes face: modelled ears and nose, applied eyes, incised facial lines.	Late

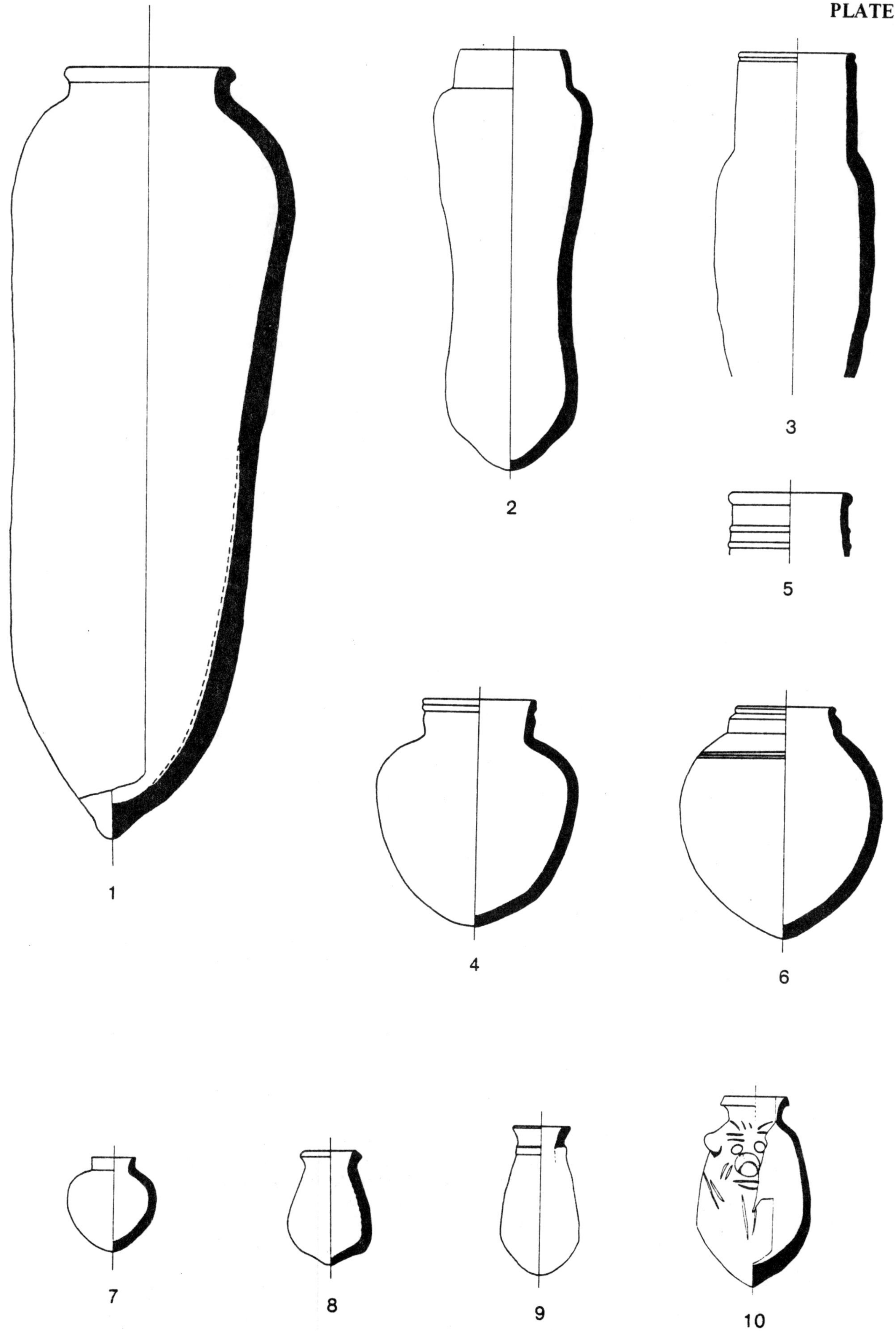

PLATE XVI

1

2

3

5

4

6

7

8

9

10

Plate XVII: Holemouth jars (1-2), Widemouth jars (3-11)   Scale 1:4

Type Number & Provenience	Description	Date
1. 7MP814 Square III Locus 45 Level IIC	Holemouth jar. Alluvial clay, organic temper, heavily fired, slightly warped. Fabric: red (10R 5/8), black core. Surface: very thin red slip (10R 4/8) exterior, matte. Wheel made. Unmodelled direct rim.	Late
2. 7MP33 Square V Locus 10 Level IIA	Holemouth jar. Alluvial clay, organic temper, moderately fired. Surface: light red (2.5YR 6/6), red core (10R 5/8), matte, wet smoothed. Wheel made. Unmodelled direct rim.	Late
3. 7MP76 Square I Locus 1 Level IIB	Widemouth jar. Pinkish marl clay, fine grit temper, moderately fired. Fabric: light red (2.5YR 6/6). Surface: pinkish white (7.5YR 8/2), matte, wet smoothed. Wheel made. Unmodelled direct rim, diverging sharply, groove at corner point.	Late
4. 7MP95 Square I Locus 1 Level IIB	Widemouth jar. Alluvial clay, organic temper, moderately fired, black core. Fabric: red (10R 5/8). Surface: red slip (10R 4/8) exterior, matte. Wheel made. Modelled lip rim.	Late
5. 7MP16 Square I Locus 1 Level IIB	Widemouth jar. Alluvial clay, organic temper, lightly fired. Fabric: reddish yellow (5YR 6/6). Surface: red wash (10R 4/8) exterior, matte. Wheel made. Round base with bump in middle, modelled lip rim.	Late
6. 7MP117 Square IV Level III	Widemouth jar. Alluvial clay, organic temper, moderately fired, warped. Surface: red (10R 5/6), matte, wet smoothed. Wheel made. Modelled lip rim, folded over.	Late
7. 7MP233 Square II Locus 4, Pot H Level IIA	Widemouth jar. Alluvial clay, organic temper, moderately fired, darker core. Surface: red (10R 5/8), matte, wet smoothed. Wheel made. Applied ring base below which round bottom of vessel projects, modelled direct rim, flaring.	Late
8. 7MP657 Square IV Level III	Widemouth jar. Dense alluvial clay, white grit temper (shell?), some organic temper, moderately fired. Fabric: weak red (10R 4/4). Surface: white slip (10YR 8/2) exterior and over rim, matte to slightly lustrous. Wheel made. Modelled lip rim.	Third Intermediate
9. 7MP88 Square I Locus 1 Level IIB	Widemouth jar. Alluvial clay, coarse organic temper, moderately fired, black core. Surface: red (10R 5/8), matte, rough. Wheel made. Modelled lip rim.	Late
10. 7MP231 Square III Locus 21 Level I	Widemouth jar. Alluvial clay, organic temper, moderately fired. Fabric: reddish yellow (5YR 6/6), red core (10R 5/8). Surface: red slip (10R 5/8) exterior and interior, matte. Wheel made. Modelled lip rim; two loop handles pressed against rim and vessel wall.	Late
11. 7MP624 Square VI Locus 41 Level IIB	Widemouth jar. Dense alluvial clay, fine grit and organic temper, moderately fired. Fabric: shades of red (10R 4/8 to 4/2), black core. Surface: slipped, varying from red (10R 4/6) to very pale brown (10YR 7/4) exterior and over rim, matte. Wheel made. Modelled lip rim.	Third Intermediate

PLATE XVII

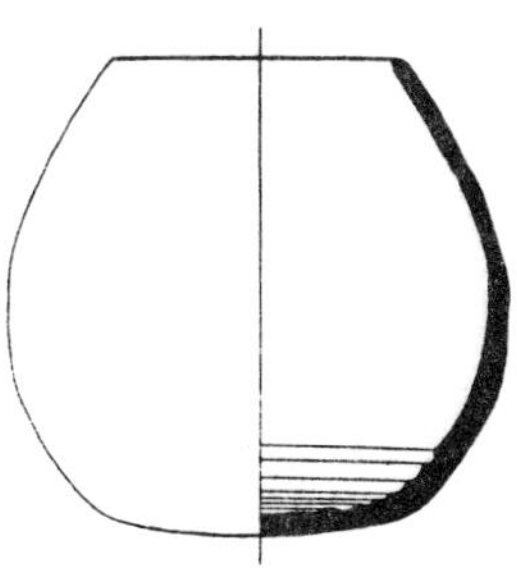

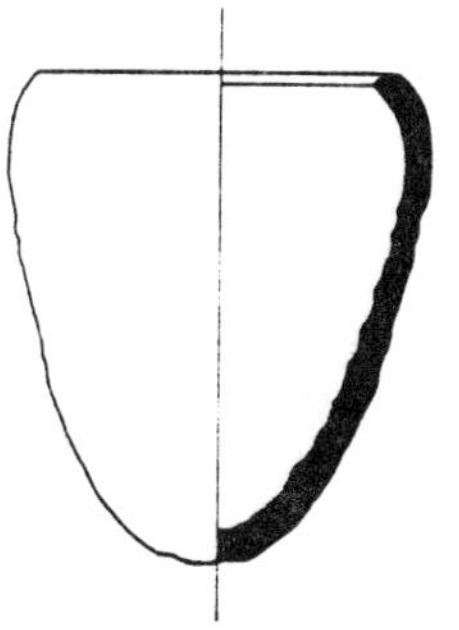

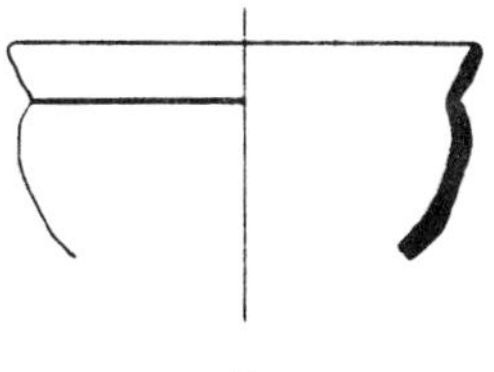

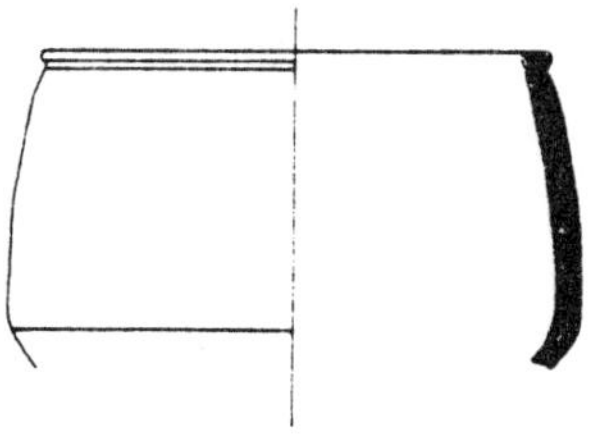

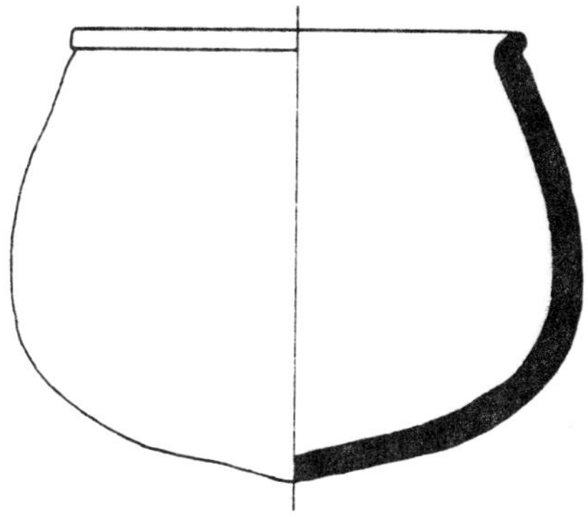

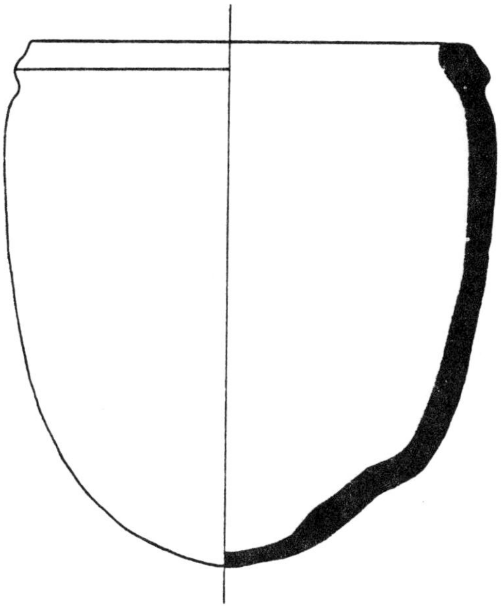

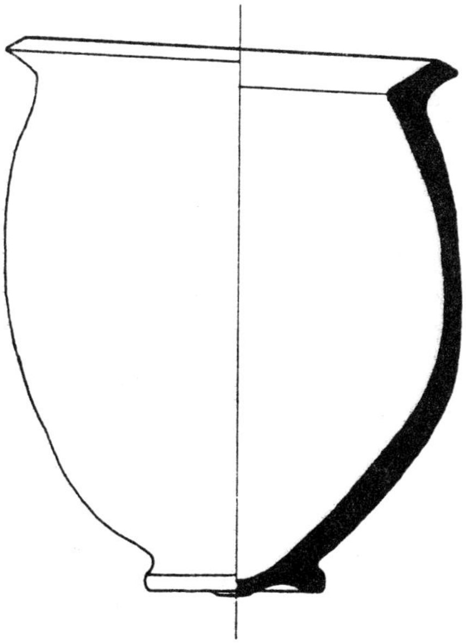

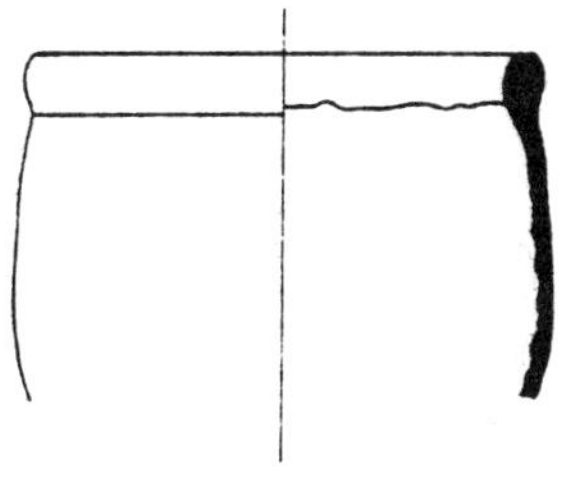

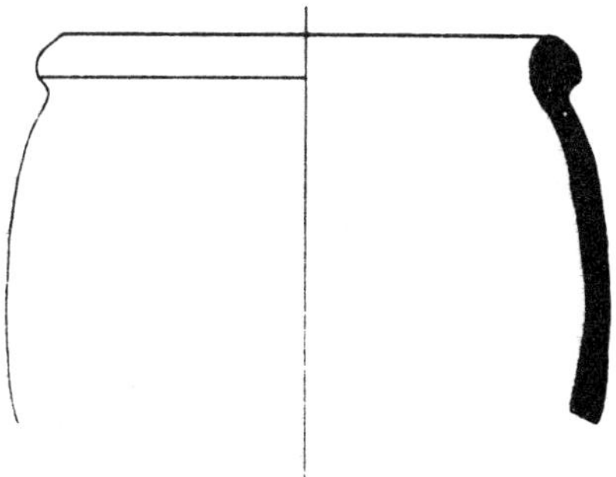

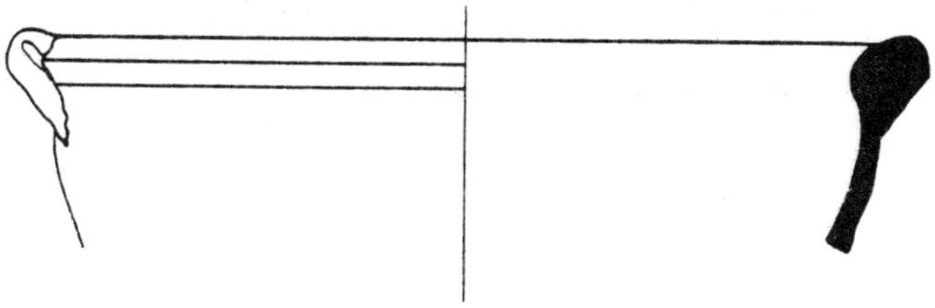

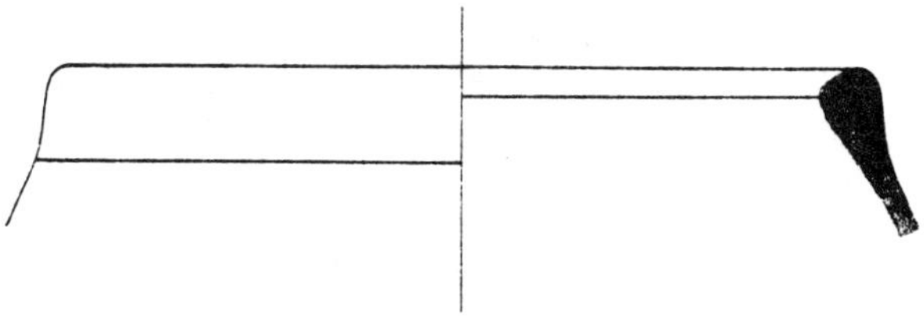

Plate XVIII: Large jars (1-4) and Bottles (5-7)   Scale 1:4 (1-3, 5-7) and 1:8 (4)

Type Number & Provenience	Description	Date
1. 7MP648 Square VI Locus 41 Level IIB	Large jar. Alluvial clay, finely divided organic temper, moderately fired, gray core. Fabric: reddish brown (5YR 5/4) to red (10R 5/8). Surface: light red slip (10R 6/8) exterior, matte. Wheel made. Modelled lip rim, folded; 2 ribbed loop handles below rim.	Third Intermediate
2. 7MP563 Square IV Pot B Level IIA	Large jar. Alluvial clay, organic temper, moderately fired. Surface: red (10R 5/8), matte, wet smoothed. Wheel made. Unmodelled direct rim diverging sharply, 2 ribbed oval loop handles.	Late
3. 7MP457 Square II Locus 4, Pot K Level IIA	Large jar. Alluvial clay, grit (grog?) and organic temper. Surface: red (10R 6/8), matte, wet smoothed. Body coil built, rim finished on wheel. Round base with bump, modelled lip rim, folded over.	Late
4. 7MP45 Square V Locus 13 Level IIA-B	Large jar. Alluvial clay, organic temper, moderately fired. Fabric: red (10R 5/8). Surface: red wash (10R 4/8) exterior, matte. Hand made. Base may have been begun on wheel. Pointed base concave at tip, modelled lip rim; ribbing on shoulder, around middle of body.	Late
5. 7MP780 Square III Locus 45 Level IIC	Bottle. Alluvial clay, organic temper, moderately fired. Fabric: yellowish red (5YR 5/8). Surface: red wash (10R 4/8) exterior, matte. Wheel made. Modelled lip rim.	Late
6. 7MP271 Square III Locus 44 Level IIA + Square V Locus 14 Level IIA	Bottle. Marl clay, fine grit temper. Surface: white (2.5Y 8/2), pink core (5YR 7/4), matte, wet smoothed. Wheel made. Disc base, loop handle, modelled direct rim. Two bands smeary reddish brown paint (2.5YR 4/6) around body.	Late
7. 7MP6 Square V Locus 43 Level IIC	Pilgrim bottle. Marl clay, grit temper, moderately fired. Exterior surface: pink (5YR 7/4), matte, wet smoothed. Probably mold made body, mold or wheel made rim, hand finished handles. Body incised with spiral on both halves, modelled direct rim.	Late

PLATE XVIII

Plate XIX: Amphorae Scale 1:4

Type Number & Provenience	Description	Date
1. 7MP39 Square VI Locus 42 Level IIA	Amphora. Marl clay, grit temper, moderately fired. Surface: pink (5YR 8/4) to reddish yellow (5YR 7/6), mottled, matte, wet smoothed. Wheel made. Pointed base, 2 ribbed loop handles, modelled direct rim.	Late
2. 7MP72 Square I Locus 1 Level IIB	Amphora. Marl clay, fine grit temper, moderately fired. Fabric: pink (5YR 7/4). Surface: pink (7.5YR 8/4), matte, wet smoothed. Wheel made. Modelled direct rim.	Late
3. 7MP459 Square III Locus 44 Level IIA	Amphora. Marl clay, grit temper, moderately fired. Fabric: red (2.5YR 5/8), uneven gray core. Surface: pinkish-white slip (7.5YR 8/2) exterior, slightly lustrous. Wheel made. Modelled lip rim. Decorated with freely painted lines on rim, neck, and handle in red (2.5YR 5/8) and brown (2.5YR 2.5/2).	Late
4. 7MP471 Square VI Locus 42 Level IIA	Amphora. Marl clay, fine grit temper, moderately fired. Surface: reddish yellow (5YR 7/6), matte, wet smoothed. Wheel made. Tapering to ring base foot. Decorated with painted bands, red to dark reddish brown (10R 4/8 to 2.5YR 3/4).	Late
5. 7MP26 Square V Locus 40 Level IIA	Amphora. Marl clay, fine grit temper, moderately fired. Fabric: light red (2.5YR 6/8). Surface: reddish yellow (5YR 7/6), matte, wet smoothed. Wheel made. Knob base with slight depression at tip.	Late

PLATE XIX

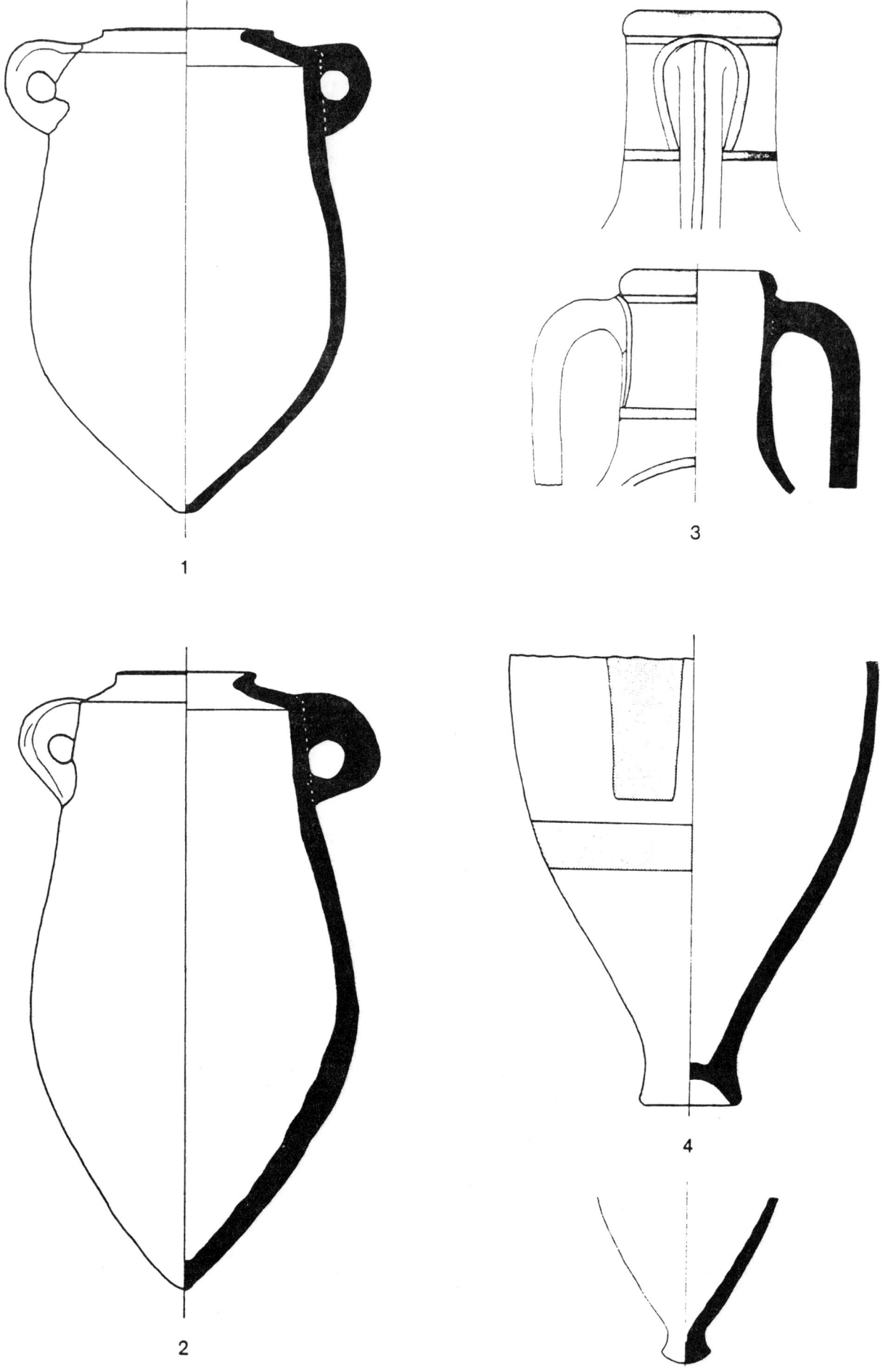

Plate XX: Lids (1-7), Burners (8-9)   Scale 1:4

Type Number & Provenience	Description	Date
1. 7MP56 Square II Surface	Lid. Alluvial clay, finely divided organic temper, heavily fired. Surface: red (10R 4/8), matte, fire clouded, wet smoothed. Wheel made, top pinched off by hand. Unmodelled direct rim.	Late
2. 7MP707 Square V Locus 43 Level IIC	Lid. Alluvial clay, organic temper, moderately fired. Fabric: red (2.5YR 5/8). Surface: red (10R 5/8), matte, wet smoothed. Wheel made, top string cut. Uneven, unmodelled direct rim.	Late
3. 7MP758 Square I Locus 1 Level IIB	Lid. Alluvial clay, organic temper, moderately fired. Surface: light reddish brown (5YR 6/4), matte, wet smoothed. Wheel made, top string cut. Modelled lip rim with interior projection.	Late
4. 7MP765 Square I Locus 1 Level IIB	Lid. Alluvial clay, organic temper, moderately fired, black core. Surface: yellowish red (5YR 5/6), matte, wet smoothed. Wheel made, round top finished by hand. Modelled lip rim with vertical projection.	Late
5. 7MP312 Square II Surface or Level I	Lid. Alluvial clay, organic and some grit temper, possibly crushed limestone or shell, moderately fired. Fabric: red (2.5YR 5/8 to 10R 5/8), black core. Surface: red (2.5YR 5/8), matte, wet smoothed. Wheel made, upper surface scraped. Modelled lip rim, interior of rim grooved, interior edge blackened.	Late
6. 7MP635 Square V Locus 15 Level IIA-B	Lid. Alluvial clay, organic temper, moderately fired. Fabric: red (10R 5/8). Surface: light red (10R 6/8), matte. Hand made. Top surface scraped and hole pierced through middle, unmodelled direct rim.	Late
7. 7MP38 Square III Locus 44 Level IIA	Lid. Alluvial clay, coarse organic temper, lightly fired. Surface: red (10R 4/8), black core, matte, rough; underside pitted and cracked; surface mottled and stained. Hand made.	Late
8. 7MP411 Square VI Locus 34 Level I	Burner. Alluvial clay, finely divided organic temper, lightly fired. Fabric: reddish yellow (5YR 6/8) to red (10R 5/8), black core. Surface: red slip (10R 4/8) exterior, slightly lustrous, burnished. Traces burning on interior of rim. Wheel made, probably in sections. Unmodelled direct rim.	Late
9. 7MP18 Sqaure I Locus 1 Level IIB	Burner. Alluvial clay, organic temper, lightly fired. Fabric: light reddish brown (5YR 6/4). Surface: red wash (10R 4/8) exterior, matte. Wheel made, probably in sections. Unmodelled direct rim.	Late

PLATE XX

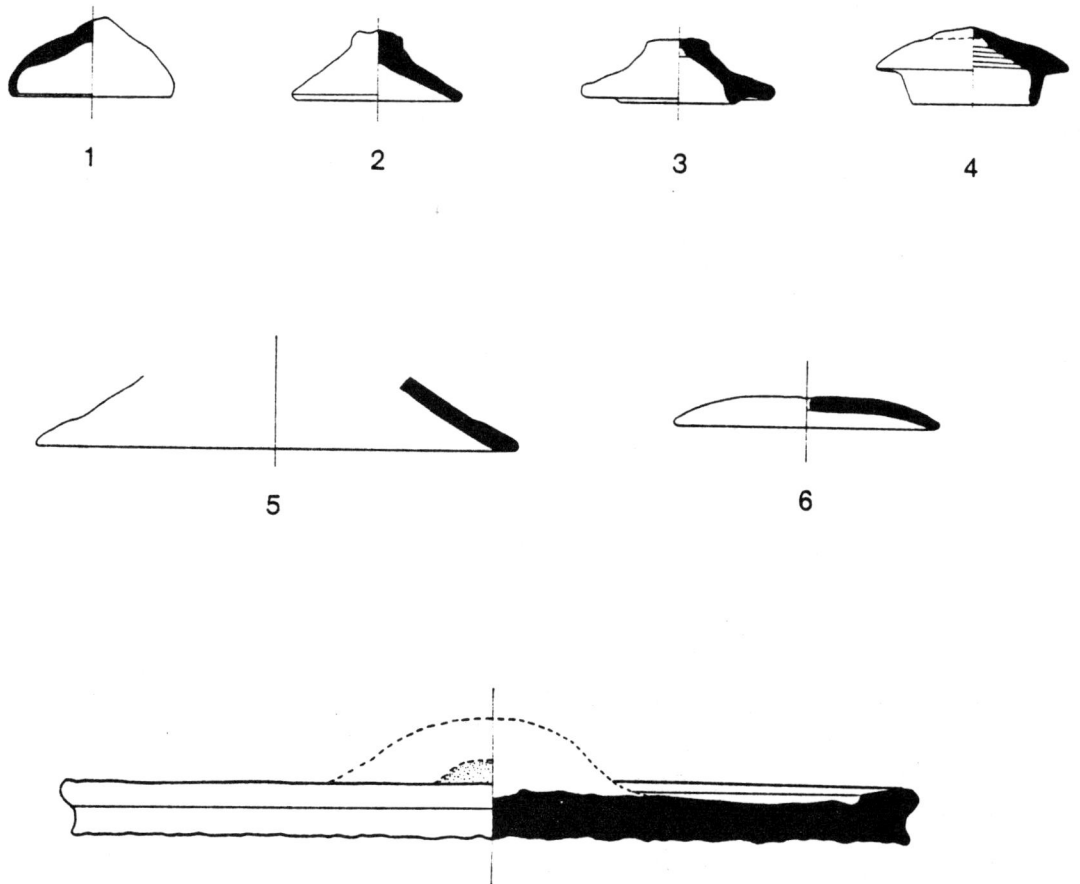

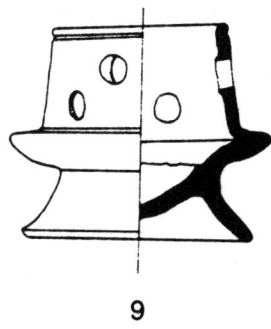

Plate XXI: Stands (1-3), Miniatures (4-5), Theriomorphic vessel (6) Scale 1:4 (1-3), 1:2 (4-6)

Type Number & Provenience	Description	Date
1. 7MP104 Square III Locus 26 Level IIA	Ring stand. Alluvial clay, organic temper, moderately fired. Surface: red (10R 5/8), matte, wet smoothed. Wheel made. Modelled lip rim on base, unmodelled direct rim on top.	Late
2. 7MP789 Square III Locus 21 Level I	Stand. Alluvial clay, organic temper, moderately fired. Fabric: red (10R 5/8). Surface: red slip (10R 4/8) exterior of stand base, interior and exterior of bowl, matte. Wheel made, probably in two halves. Modelled lip rim, ledge.	Late
3. 7MP11 Square I Locus 1 Level IIB	Stand. Alluvial clay, coarse organic temper, moderately fired, black core. Surface: red (10R 4/8), mottled, matte. Underside coarse and pitted. Hand made. Supports end in modelled direct rims.	Late
4. 7MP60 Square III Locus 5 East wall Level I	Miniature bowl. Alluvial clay, organic temper, moderately fired. Surface: red (10R 4/6), matte, wet smoothed. Probably wheel made. Modelled direct rim, profile distorted.	Late
5. 7MP473 Square V Locus 43 Level IIC	Miniature pilgrim bottle. Alluvial clay, fine organic temper, moderately fired. Surface: red wash (10R 5/8) exterior, matte. Hand made, almost solid.	Late
6. 7MP599 Square V Locus 43 Level IIC	Theriomorphic vessel: bird. Alluvial clay, organic temper, lightly fired. Surface: reddish yellow (5YR 6/8), matte, wet smoothed. Hand made, hole cut through back of body and pierced through neck. 2 applied wings and applied or modelled tail, head missing.	Late

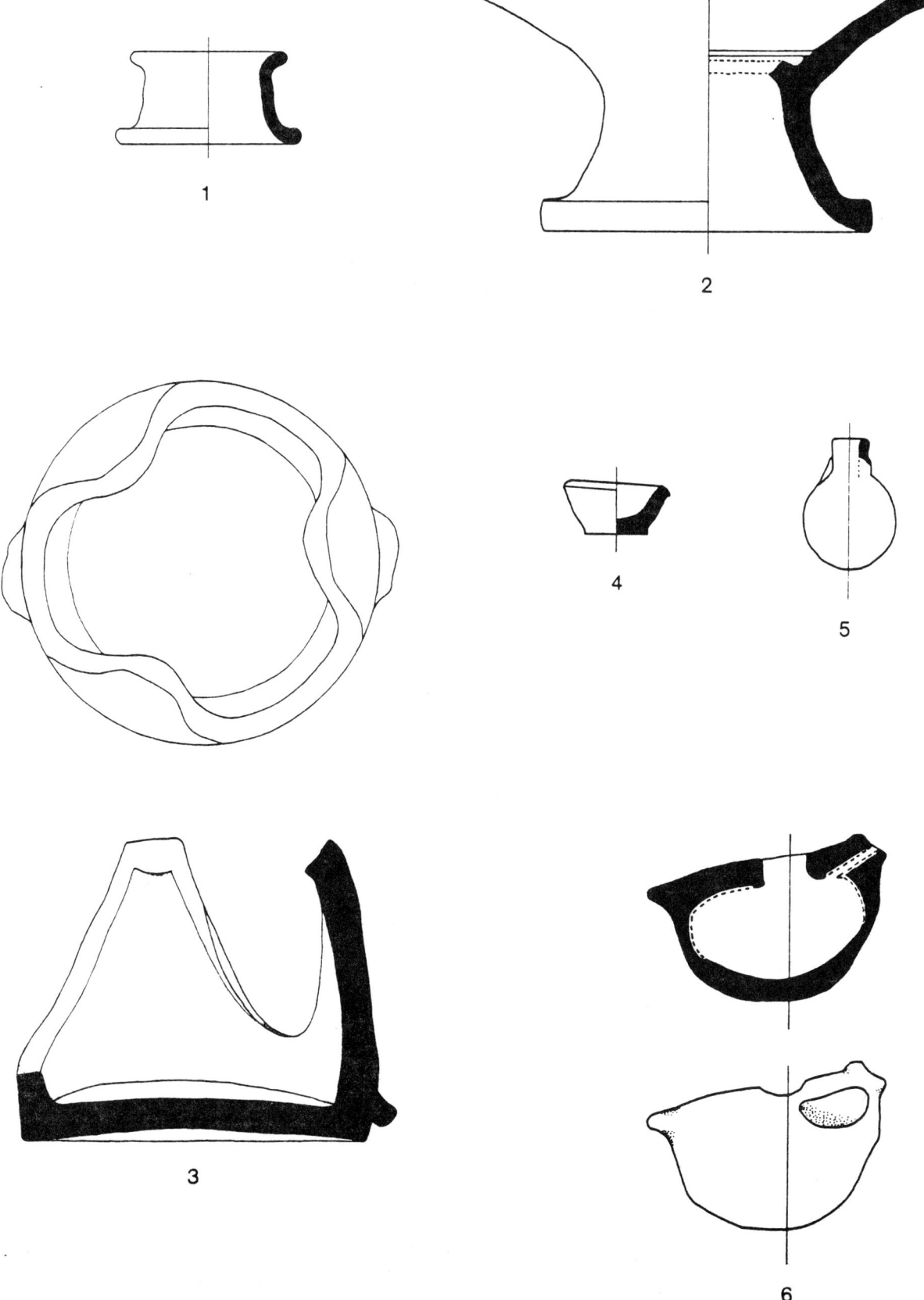

PLATE XXI

Plate XXII

Type Number & Provenience	Description	Date
1. 7MPX15 Square IV Level III	False spout of stirrup jar. Light colored fabric. Concentric circles in lustrous red and black paint flanked by reserved triangles. L = 5.4 cm.	Late Helladic III A
2. 7MPX22 Square V Locus 43 Level IIC	Shoulder fragment of oinochoe. Cream slipped fabric. At join of neck: tongues; below: remains of three water birds. Decoration in black paint with added red on middle bird. Silhouette with details reserved. H = 4.2, L = 6.2 cm.	"Rhodian" 625-600 B.C.

PLATE XXII

Plate XXIII

Type Number & Provenience	Description	Date
1. 7MPX35 Square V Locus 33 Level IID	Shoulder and neck of closed vessel. Light fabric with thick, glossy, cream slip. Paint firing orange to reddish brown. On neck: two felines flanking a bird or siren. On shoulder: sphinx, palmette flanked by two swans. Details incised, added red on bird (siren), neck and wing of swans, alternate fronds of palmette. H = 8.0, Neck diameter = 9.0 cm.	North Ionian 580-560 B.C.
2. 7MPX41 Square III Locus 45 Level IIC	Shoulder fragment of neck amphora with traces of handle attachment. Light fabric with cream slip; decoration in paint firing to red. Goat leaping to right with head turned back. Ground line and two broad bands below. Silhouette with reserved details and outline technique. H = 11.5, Maximum diameter = 24.0 cm.	"Rhodian" 580-560 B.C.

PLATE XXIII

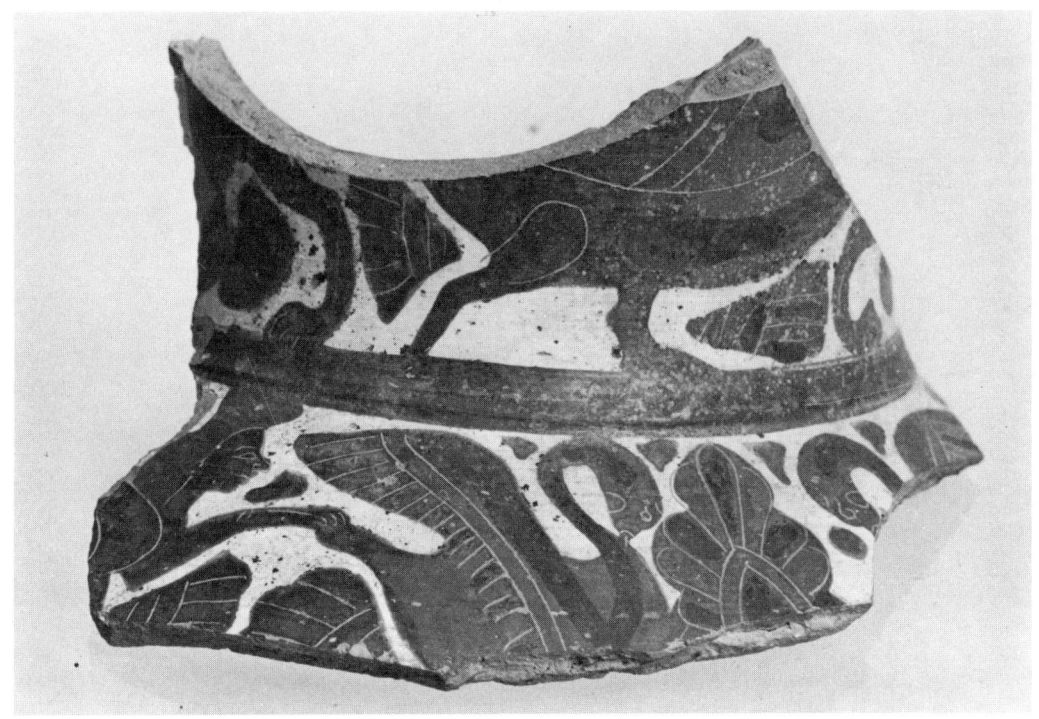

Plate XXIV

Type Number & Provenience	Description	Date
1-2. 7MPX29 Square VI Level IIC and 3. 8MPX19 Square IX Level IIC	Three non-joining shoulder fragments of neck amphora with traces of handle attachments. Light fabric with cream slip; decoration in paint firing to reddish brown. On either side of vessel a goat leaping to right. Plate XXIV:1 — belly and foreleg of first goat; Plate XXIV:2 — part of horn of first goat and rear leg of second goat; Plate XXIV:3 — foreleg and tip of horn of second goat. Ground line and two broad bands below. Silhouette with reserved details and outline technique. Plate XXIV:1 — H = 11.5 cm. Plate XXIV:2 — H = 8.8 cm. Plate XXIV:3 — H = 8.5 cm.	"Rhodian" 580-560 B.C.

PLATE XXIV

1 2

3

Plate XXV

Type Number & Provenience	Description	Date
1. 7MPX11 Square V Locus 15 Level IIA and 2. 8MPX73 Square VIII Level 1	Mouth, neck and shoulder fragment of large black figured amphora. Light red fabric with lustrous metallic black paint. On edge of lip: checkers; on neck: black band, raised fillet painted black; below: tails of two sphinxes or sirens to either side of rosette. On shoulder: remains of cock facing left; horizontal band and tongues above. Pl. XXV:1 - H = 5.8, Diameter = 30.0 cm. (Same as Pl. XXVII:1) Pl. XXV:2 - H = 4.5 cm.	Clazomenian 550-540 B.C.
3. 7MPX27 Square VI Surface	Body fragment from closed, black figured vessel. Remains of two friezes separated by thinned glaze line. Above: feline striding to right. Below: shoulder of herbivore grazing to left. Details incised; added red on shoulder of herbivore. H = 5.3 cm.	Attic 580-570 B.C.

1

2

3

Plate XXVI

Type Number & Provenience	Description	Date
1. 8MPX12 Surface north of excavation (brought in by workman)	Body fragment from panel amphora. Feet and legs of male moving to right; between legs, a bit of drapery. Glazed black below panel; some abrasion. Incised for details. Added red bands below panel. H = 6.7 cm.	Attic 525-500 B.C. (?)
2. 8MPX62 Square X Surface	Squat lekythos, bottom half. Seated sphinx facing right, with forepaw raised. Thinned glaze for inner details. Wing in relief line decoration. H = 4.5 cm. Base diameter = 5.1 cm.	Attic Late 5th-early 4th century B.C.

PLATE XXVI

Plate XXVII   Scale 1:2

Type Number & Provenience	Description	Date
1. 7MPX11 Square V Locus 15 Level IIA-B	(Same as Plate XXV:1)	Clazomenian 550-540 B.C.
2. 7MPX3 Square V Surface	Lekythos mouth and neck; handle root preserved. Light red fabric with metallic black paint.	Attic 5th century B.C.
3. 7MPX6 Square V Surface	Body of small olpe. Light red fabric with black metallic paint.	Attic ca. 350 B.C.

PLATE XXVII

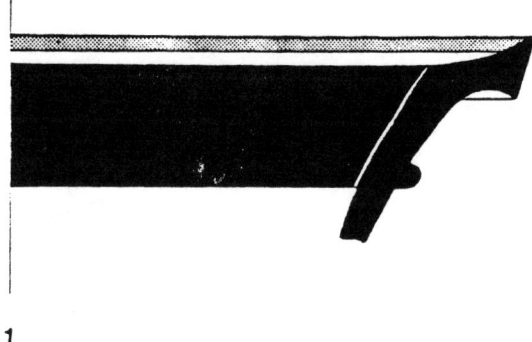

1

2

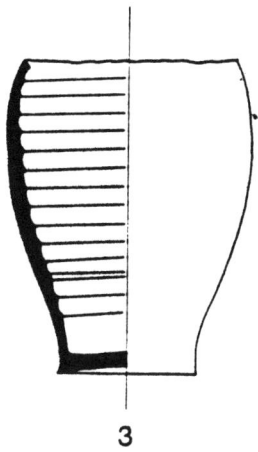

3

PLATE XXVIII

Plate XXVIII. Faience amulets: *udjat* amulets (1-6), Shu amulets (7-8), Thoeris amulets (9-10), falcon amulet (11), ram amulet (12), Thoth amulet (13).

PLATE XXIX

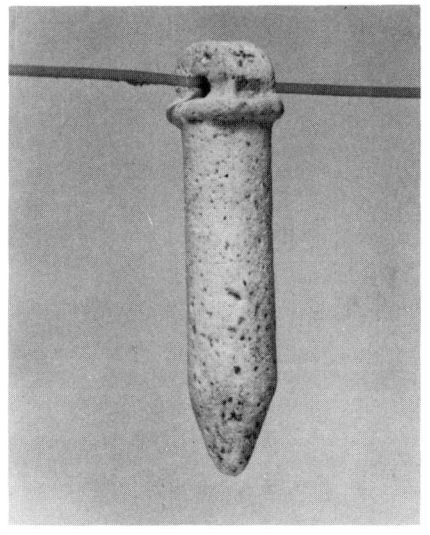

1

2

3

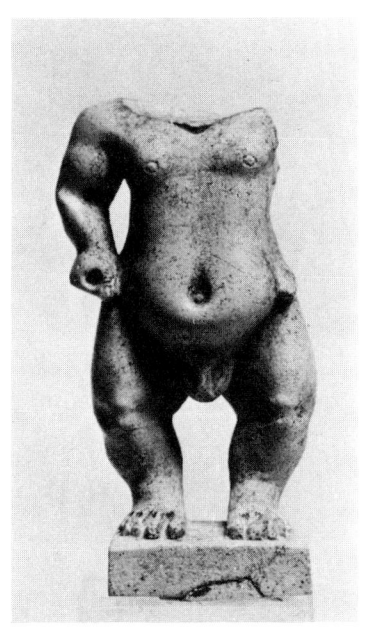

4

5

Plate XXIX. Faience amulets: *uadj* amulets (1-2), Pataikos amulets (3-4), Bes amulet (5).

PLATE XXX

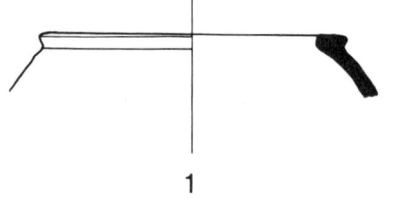

1

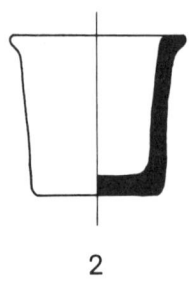

2

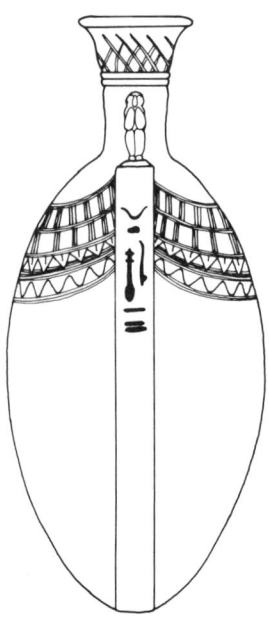 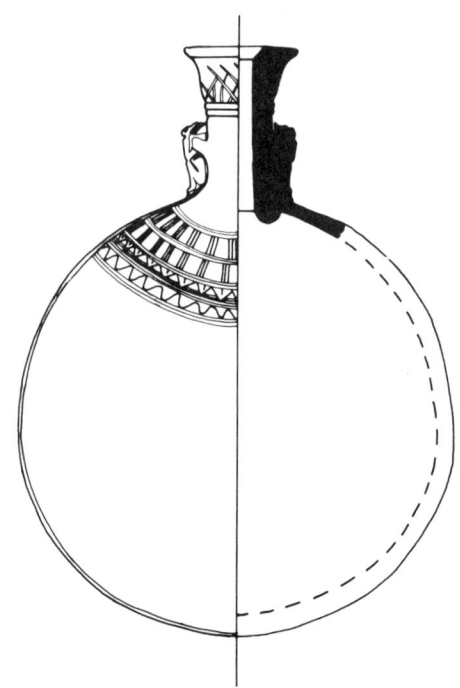

3

Plate XXX. Faience vessels.

PLATE XXXI

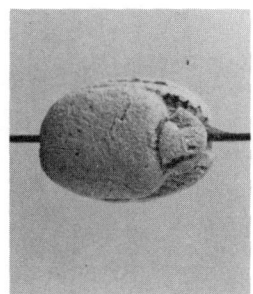 

1

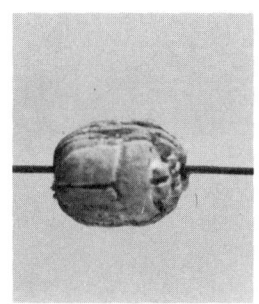 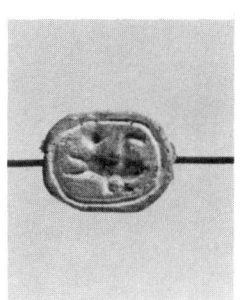

2

3

Plate XXXI. Scarabs.

PLATE XXXII

Plate XXXII. Terracotta moulds for amulets.

PLATE XXXIII

1

2

3

4

Plate XXXIII. Terracotta ram figurine fragments.

PLATE XXXIV

1

2

3

Plate XXXIV. "Tokens," grinder, and "weights" (1); Mitannian cylinder seal (2-3).

Plate XXXV. Third Intermediate Period relief fragment.